RED-HEADED STEPCHILD

Beyond the Beatings

By
Dr. Jason Powell

Table of Contents

Sentencing

The judge stared across his bench at me, stone-faced and silent. My heart leapt inside my chest. I could feel the tension growing all around the courtroom. Dozens of eyes were upon me, but only the judge's made me shudder. My breath felt trapped within my lungs. Any second now this man, this keeper of the law, the kind of authority I had been taught my entire life to fear, would rain down his judgement on me. Me? I'd been in and out of courtrooms my entire life, but this was my first time the outcome would actually matter to me. And the stakes had never been higher than today. Anxiously, I peered over at my three frightened sisters sitting there in the courtroom, awaiting what this man had to say. I could see their tiny nervous fingers fidgeting in their laps. His words would not only affect my life, but theirs as well. I felt a cold sweat gather on my back. I started to wonder why there was a bailiff in every courtroom with a loaded firearm. Do they ever use these in a courtroom? Was this truly necessary for our courtroom? Why was he there? What was he there to do? Suddenly the judge stood from his seat and began walking towards me. I could feel my eyes growing wider with every second. This was it. I struggled to keep my composure. In my mind, a single thought remained:

How did my life come to this moment?

A Start to My End

To explain my history, I need to go back to my parents' stories. My mother was a troubled teen who spent very little time at home. She was a runaway who got involved with drugs, alcohol, and all the wrong people at a very young age. She was an overweight, ginger girl with freckles, and major insecurities. Like most teenage girls, she loved music, movies, and enjoying time with her friends. Though she was full of laughter and fun, she didn't know how to love herself, value herself, or fight for her own self-worth. At fifteen years old, she found herself in a relationship with an older man— my stepfather Warner.

Warner was a twenty-five-year-old man when he began his involvement with my mother. He came from a good family and was raised with all the luxuries and privileges a child could ask for. He'd been given a good education, taught manners, and to have a good work ethic. However, he decided to trade all of his privileges in for a life of drugs, alcohol, fighting, and crime. No matter what his parents did to ensure his success, Warner was a constant problem for his family. They eventually disowned him after his attempt to kill them by opening fire with an assault rifle into their home.

I imagine my mom was attracted to the confidence, power, and swagger that Warner undoubtedly portrayed. Warner probably loved the idea of an insecure girl swooning over him. Their relationship most likely blossomed through endless nights of fun and laughter, polluted with drugs and alcohol.

After two years of dating my mother, Warner was arrested and sentenced to four years in Chino State Prison. It turned out he had been sleeping with another young girl as well during this time. Despite being underage herself, my mother never reported their relationship and so he was only arrested and charged with one case of child molestation.

About two years into Warner's imprisonment, my mother started dating another man for a short time. As a result of their time together, I was conceived. When my mom learned of her pregnancy, she broke up with the man, never telling him anything about the pregnancy. Years later, she told me that the man had too many hopes and dreams to be tied down to a family and so she never told him. She feared she would be the cause of de-railing him from his bright, prospective future. This man continued on in life without ever knowing of my existence.

Out of pure fear, and since she never officially ended her relationship with Warner, my mother neglected to ever tell Warner about her extracurricular relationship or her pregnancy.

Warner served his four years as mandated by the courts. During this time in prison, he evolved into the worst typical image of a dangerous inmate. He was angry, abusive, and covered in tattoos. He also spent a lot of time lifting weights and so he was significantly bigger and stronger.

Once Warner's sentencing was complete, he was released from prison. Having burned all bridges with his own family, he only had one person left in his life: my mom. And after four years of letters filled with promises of a life together, my mom eagerly awaited his arrival.

When Warner came home to my mom, he never expected to find me, the "one-year-old, little b*stard who was conceived behind his back." Angered by my existence, he decided that I was garbage and did not belong in his home. I don't know how true the story is, but he told me several different times throughout my childhood that they tossed me into a Safeway dumpster to get rid of me, but I cried until someone heard me. The Child Protective Services (CPS) had ultimately brought me back to my mother. I don't understand how this could possibly be true, but it was a long time ago, the early 1980's, and my life is full of many strange occurrences.

Warner was over six feet tall with a shaved head, a thick red beard, and was covered from the neck down with tattoos. These tattoos were images of Hitler, "White-Pride," and explicit scenes of half animal/half human creatures performing sexual acts, all over his body. I always sensed his bright blue/grey eyes were not windows to a soul as he appeared to look through me. He was strong, intimidating, vulgar, and always looked angry.

He hated me. Absolutely despised my presence. He decided the moment he saw me that I would never be his son, and so began my life of torment. He started by renaming me Jake Dawson rather than my real name of Jason Powell. It seemed a means of making me his property. Although he renamed me "Jake" he seldom referred to me by this name. I was almost always referred to as some sort of horrible racist, sexist, or derogatory slur.

I was barely a year old when he came home and so he was my dad. In my dad's (Warner's) house, I was not allowed to speak unless spoken to or granted permission to do so by him. If I did speak out of turn, I would be hit in the mouth or shoved face first into a wall. This was his way of controlling both my mother and me.

Instead of speaking with words, I was taught to speak using American Sign Language (ASL). Warner was fluent in ASL and my mother was not far behind in her understanding. And so, teaching me was no more difficult than teaching any child their first language. Because I had never seen anything different, this seemed completely normal to me. Neither of my parents were hard of hearing nor deaf. This was nothing more than a tool for Warner to enslave my mother and me. By taking our voices away, he could literally control what we said and who we said it to. Warner also utilized this as a way for him to get away with criminal activities. By the time I was five years old, he was able to utilize my sign language to his benefits. When people asked questions or the police came looking for him, our family was suddenly deaf.

Every time we heard pounding on the front door, in a panicked rush, my dad would whisper at me as he ran to hide. "It's the police, get rid of them. We are not here!"

As he and my mother quickly vanished to the back of the house, I would slowly open the door, just enough for my face to squeeze through. I recall one time when two policemen were standing there fully dressed in their uniforms. They always had the same booming knock, the same boxy shirts, and the same guns, batons, and handcuffs. I was scared whenever they came to our house. I was made to believe that the police were bad and only came around to try and hurt us. They were there to steal my parents away from me. It was almost always the same scenario every time they came to our house.

"Hello, is your dad home?"

I would nervously open the door a slight bit more and begin to sign to them in sign language. My hands shaking as I frantically signed in hopes that they would leave.

"I'm sorry, my dad is not here."

The policemen would almost always be noticeably caught off guard. They would point into the house while speaking slower and louder as if I would now be able to hear them.

"Is anyone else here? Are your parents' home?"

I would shake my head "no." The policeman would then walk back to their car where they would sit for what felt like an eternity. Once the door was shut, my parents would run to the front window where they would smash their faces up against the black spray-painted glass to spy on the policemen. My parents had scraped away small holes in the painted glass to peek through whenever there was any movement outside.

My mother loved me dearly, but she feared Warner. He was extremely abusive in every way imaginable to her. His constant threats of killing us bound my mother into a life of fear and torment. He made us believe that we were worthless pieces of garbage that he was more than willing to kill at any time. We were "fat, disgusting, and pathetic." No one could want us. In his presence, I always felt like a worthless disappointment to the human race. By forcing us to speak only ASL, he essentially ensured our captivity within his house. He wanted to make sure that we remained under his control. Starting as early as four and five years old, my parents would leave me home alone for days at a time, leaving me locked up, abandoned, and alone in our house. When I was left alone, I remember crying uncontrollably. I lived in fear, feeling isolated and hated with no one to share my feelings with.

Whenever my family did go out in public, my dad would pre-script everything we were "allowed" to say. This helped to guarantee that we would never speak about him or any of the things that were happening in our home. This hindered our ability to make friends, correspond with acquaintances, or even have basic normal dialogue with strangers we encountered. In short, we were isolated and alone as his prisoners.

I did know how to speak, but always feared having my voice heard. When in public away from my dad, I would secretly try to talk to people, but it was always done with extreme caution. Even when I did find the courage to speak with others, I was scared. I would fidget nervously as I looked around to make sure he would not see me. My voice would tremble, and my heart would pound from the fear of breaking his rules, as I attempted simple conversations with others.

My mom would secretly talk with me when my dad was not home. She would sit with me on her lap as she caressed my head, played with my hair, and whispered to me as if she had permanently quieted her vocal cords. Sometimes, she would read me a children's story, while other times we would laugh together from her jokes and funny stories. I loved my mom so much, even though she couldn't protect me. I know that she loved me because she would cry out against Warner whenever he would do things to me. It always broke my heart more to see my mom's pain when he hurt me, than the physical pain he was inflicting upon me.

There were times when my mother would attempt to fight back against him. This always resulted in highly abusive, loud, and scary fights. My mother would fight against him the best she could, but he would always win. Things would fly throughout the house as she tried to escape his violent beatings.

As they screamed at the top of their lungs at each other, I would hide in fear of being brought into the fight.

No matter what the cause of the fight, he would always find a way to direct the screaming and fighting towards me. It was somehow always my fault. He made sure that I knew I was the reason for their fighting. The message was that if my mother had not ever had me, things would have been better for both of them. After his rage would turn towards me, I would hide myself in the corner and cry quietly in fear. It was my fault; I ruined their lives. His fights with my mom usually ended with him throwing her to the ground. He would sit on top of her, pin her wrists and feet to the floor and then yell at me to "get the f*ck out of here."

Each time, when these fights finally came to end, Warner would leave the house. My mother would come into my room with her face swollen and covered in blood, snot, and tears. She would grab my hand and then drag me down the street with her. We would run to the end of the street and then into an alleyway or behind a building, basically, anywhere we could find to hide so that he could not find us. Trying to hide her pain, she would whisper to me with the little breath she had left in her. Through her deep sobs of emotional and physical pain, she would tell me what to do.

"Quickly get behind the dumpster and shut up! We need to hide."

As darkness fell over the sky, we would curl up into a little ball behind the dumpster on the cold ground to try and sleep. The cold air would make my ears and nose ache. I would curl up into a little ball inside of whatever I could use for a blanket and then make a small vent for the freezing cold air to make its way into my nose. Often, as we lay there shivering from the cold and shaking in fear, I could hear my mom crying and praying to God.

"Dear God, help me break free. Help me get away. Give me strength or let me die."

Under my breath, I would quietly mimic her words as she prayed, changing only the last part.

"Dear God, help us break free. Help us get away. Give us strength. Please don't let her die."

I would hide my face from her in shame as I cried myself to sleep. Some nights, we could hear him racing his truck up and down the streets screaming out for us.

As the sun came up in the morning, my mother would wake me up to go home.

"It's time for us to go home. He will be worried if he wakes up and we are not there."

I couldn't understand why we would leave if we were just going to go home again afterwards, but I did as I was told. Most mornings, we would get home to find my dad passed out in the living room. Glass would be all over the floor from bottles thrown across the house. This was a normal routine and so I knew better than to say anything. The stench of the filthy, cold, dark house would burn my nose as the morning light beamed in when we entered. We would sneak around the house to the back door to enter because we were never permitted to use the front door. Light would creep into the house, waking him as we entered.

Most mornings, he would quickly get up off the floor to greet us with an uncomfortable hug before telling us how worried he was for us.

"Are you guys OK? It's dangerous out there for you guys. I was worried sick about you. Don't ever leave here like that again."

We were made to believe that we were not safe outside of his house. No one could ever like us, and no one would ever want us around. He gave the impression that we were fortunate to have him because he was the only person who could ever put up with us.

"You guys are lucky I am here to take care of you. Left alone in the world, you two would die."

Other times, we would come home in the morning to find him still in a state of rage. I feared these mornings because they were always the same. It would be silent and still as we entered the house, then he would suddenly appear from out of nowhere before he would begin beating us for leaving. This became a regular routine in my life. A fight would break out, my mother and I would flee the house only to return the following day.

Intended Accidents

Warner was not my biological father. I asked my mother many times throughout my youth who my real father was, but she would never tell me. Warner was the only dad I had and so even though I was the unwanted, worthless b*stard child whom he resented; I would still call him "Dad." Most of my childhood, he wouldn't even speak directly to me. Instead, he would speak about me to my mother so that I would hear what he wanted. He would give me orders by screaming at my mother to tell "her daughter," or "her little b*tch," or "the piece of sh*t" to do whatever it was he was demanding at that moment. I would look down at the floor in fear, feeling ashamed, standing silent. I was the worthless disappointment that no one ever wanted, and who had ruined my parents' lives. It seemed that no matter how good I was or how hard I tried, it was not enough. I could not figure out what I had done to make him hate me so much. All I ever wanted was for him to accept me and possibly love me.

Even as a young child, I remember wishing for death. I thought if I died, perhaps my dad would treat my mother better and then they would live happily ever after. I knew deep down though, that if I died, nothing would really change. My dad would then just shift all of his anger and abuse solely onto my mom. I knew that if I did die, it would only be a short while before she would die too. There were times when I was so angry, I did not care anymore; I just wanted to die. I thought that perhaps my death would somehow serve as a punishment to my parents. A punishment to my dad for treating me the way he did, and a punishment to my mother for allowing it. If nothing else, at least my death would release me from the anger and hatred that was building up inside me. The pain and suffering of my thoughts and mind never let up. I felt completely alone, depressed, and angry, with no purpose and no place to belong.

Starting from my earliest memories, Warner made it beyond clear that he wished for my death. Starting around the time I was six years old, he began setting things up around our house and yard in ways that could "accidently" kill a person.

My mother told me many times not to touch anything of his because it was all dangerous. He would openly make jokes about us "accidently" dying if we touched his stuff. I remember when we were living in Westwood, California, I was around four or five years old. I had gone into my front yard to play with some old McDonald's toys. The restaurant used to give the Happy-Meals in colored plastic tubs that were shaped like different characters in boats. The plastic tub could then be used as a toy boat. I remember picking up one of my boats, and it was full of water. I dumped it out so I could play with it. Instantly, I started screaming as the liquid began burning my feet. A neighbor heard my screaming and ran over to help me. We didn't have running water at my house and so our neighbor brought me into his front yard where he began washing my feet with his garden hose. My mom ran out when she heard me screaming. She told the neighbor that we needed baking soda quickly. It was not water in my toy boat, Warner had filled it with battery acid. My mom told me I wasn't allowed to play with any of my toys in the yard anymore after that.

There was one day, I remember finding a cord hanging off the edge of our house, dangling to the ground. Warner instructed me to clean up all the trash in the yard. I did as I was told and started to collect the garbage. I began pulling on the cord when my mom ran out and stopped me. She whispered for me to quickly get away from it before my dad saw me. She told me this was a trap, an "accident" waiting to happen. Warner had placed the three-foot cube metal frame of an empty swamp cooler on the edge of the roof. If I would have pulled the cord, the heavy frame would have fallen directly onto me causing severe injury or possibly death.

Another time I was ordered to clean up the trash around the yard. I did my job as ordered, and then reported back to my dad when I had finished. Always finding fault in everything I did; he slammed my face down on the table and put a plate of trash down in front of me. He had scoured the yard looking for every scrap I had missed.

"I thought you cleaned the yard. If you did, then what is all of this? Answer me, you piece of sh*t!"

He then slammed his middle finger knuckle down on top of my head so hard that I could feel my jaw crack as my head jolted down. I had never felt that level of pain and so I immediately burst into tears.

"Eat it! Eat every f*cking bite you little b*stard. I am going to stand here and hit you every time a minute passes until you finish it."

My hands were shaking and my fingers quivering as I slowly wadded up the first plastic wrapper into a ball so that I could swallow it. I chewed on it for a minute hoping he would lose interest and leave me alone. No such luck. He didn't. He slammed the top of my head with another hit before he shoved his fingers into my mouth pushing the wrapper down my throat. I screamed out in pain as I choked and gasped for air. It took everything in me not to vomit it back up as I sat there coughing and sobbing uncontrollably. He ordered me to eat more. I grabbed the next piece of trash from the plate, which was a piece of paper. I quickly chewed on it so that I could swallow it before he hit me or made me choke again as he shoved his giant calloused fingers down my throat.

After I finished the paper, he hit me and sent me to the corner to stand in silence awaiting more punishment. As much as the beatings hurt, I was grateful not to have any more of the trash shoved down my throat. This was not the only time he had done this to me. There were many other times that he made me eat trash from the yard. Sometimes it was cigarette butts, while other times it was candy wrappers, random trash, and even occasionally dog droppings. If I didn't eat it fast enough, he would hit me so hard that I would burst into tears, sobbing uncontrollably. When this would happen, my mouth would fill with saliva making it easier for him to cram the objects down my throat.

Lassen County Detention Facility

When I was six years old, Warner was arrested again and sentenced to serve more time in prison. I don't know what he did, but I know that we had to move to Susanville because that was where he had to serve his sentence. After his release, he began taking us to "friends" houses. The houses and trailers they lived in were all similar to the places we'd lived before. They were dark, damp, and dirty. Nearly every house had all the windows covered with tin foil or painted over like ours. The people who lived in these houses were often just like us. There was usually a really mean set of parents and a filthy kid or two trying not to upset them.

I met a young girl named Alicia at one of these houses. I was excited to finally have someone to play with. Her mom was scary looking with messy black hair and a badly scarred face. But despite her appearance, Alicia's mother was usually really nice to us. However, that was not always the case. Sadly, Alicia's mom was a lot like Warner. One day while giving us food for lunch, she put some black olives on our plates. I didn't like black olives and so I gave mine to Alicia to eat. Alicia's mom began screaming at me as loud as she could.

"Why are you giving her your food? Do you want her to suck your d*ck? Do you hold your d*ck when you take a piss, then you touch her food? Should we have her suck your d*ck right now?"

Then she grabbed me up out of my chair so that I was standing. She then grabbed Alicia and threw her on the floor in front of me and told her "Suck his d*ck." Alicia burst into tears, begging her mom "No—" When my friend started crying out "No," I became petrified with fear. I began crying with her "No, please, I'm sorry." I didn't know what was happening or why she was doing this to us. I didn't understand what was wrong with giving Alicia my olives. I couldn't understand why she thought I would want Alicia to do such a thing, nor did I understand why she suddenly exploded with her dark anger at me. All I could think to do was to look down at the floor and not make eye contact, like I did with Warner. I tried to say I was sorry, but I was crying and shaking and so my words were mumbled.

Suddenly, the front door swung open. My dad raced in so fast that I could feel the whole trailer shaking with his every step. He didn't even ask what I did, he just ran over and started hitting me. No one ever said a word about what happened that day. We left their house and then I never saw my friend again.

It was common for us to leave for days at a time to go camping. Later in life I came to realize, we would go camping when Warner needed to lay low for a while, either from the police or people he'd wronged.

When we left to go camping, we would drive up Mount Shasta towards Chester, California. I hated these trips. I always thought I was going to die during the freezing cold, long and terrifying drives up the mountain. My dad would drive us up the steep mountain in his small light green truck. The cab only had a little bench seat and so he would make me lay in the bed of the truck. I would have to hide under a blue plastic tarp when we made these trips to ensure no one would see me. I would lie sideways so I could wedge myself between the wheel wells of the bed. This prevented me from sliding all over the truck as we drove. It also helped to prevent some of the pain of having to lie on the cold, hard, metal bumps that the bed of the truck was made with.

I would curl the tarp under my hands, feet, and head to protect myself from the weather. I remember, many times we encountered huge hailstorms during these drives. Hailstones would crash down on my fingers holding the tarp in place. The pain was often unbearable causing me to lose hold of a corner. The tarp would then whip about the truck exposing me to the hail. I would have to quickly sit-up to grab the tarp as it whipped against me. I didn't know what would happen if I lost his tarp, but I knew Warner's response would be worse than the pain of the hailstones. I would grab the tarp and hold it with all my might as my dad drove recklessly up the mountain as fast as he could. The hailstones would beat against my hands until I could not feel them anymore as I tried to protect my ears and face. I remember looking over the edge of the truck, only to see the cliffs on the side of the road. Most of the time we made this drive, my dad was drunk. I feared that one day, we would go over the edge and I would finally die. I would fall to my death as we fell from the cliffs of this mountain. I wished that I could beg for us not to go. I wished that I could have sat inside the cab with my parents. But I knew better than to even ask. Asking would only upset my dad and give him a reason to make things worse for me.

One night during my first-grade year, we were out camping when my dad's dog ran off.

"Jake, get in the truck. We need to find the dog. I'll drive, you scream out for him."

As we raced through the winding mountain roads, I gripped onto anything I could to keep from being thrown out of the bed of the truck. I desperately screamed for the dog in hopes of ending the search. The longer the search went on, the more he drank, and the more reckless he became. The search ultimately ended when he did drive off of the road, off the side of the mountain and into a ditch. As we went over the edge, I was launched from the bed of the truck. When I landed at the bottom, my right leg had been shattered.

I don't know how I got to the hospital or how long I was there, but I do know that I spent the next nine months with a cast starting at my crotch and ending at my toes. I also got a sizable scar across the underside of my chin. Warner only broke one of his wrists in the crash.

For years after, he would joke about having me get in the truck again so that he could "try again." He was upset that I didn't die in the crash and so he would reference my "living though the crash with only a broken leg" as a disappointment.

Whenever we drove past other car accidents, he would point out that the victims probably died "as they were supposed to."

It is interesting looking back on these events because I can now see when Warner altered his ways of abusing, manipulating, and utilizing me. My whole life up until the accident was him trying to avoid, punish, or get rid of me. After the accident, he suddenly changed to wanting to have me with him when he went out to do things.

Warner started forcing me to do illegal things for him and teaching me how not to get caught. If we were ever to get caught, I was just a minor committing the act and so there was no fear that he would go to jail for it. I would simply receive a "slap on the wrist" before being sent back home. Despite my new usefulness, I was still prohibited from looking him in the eyes, talking, or doing anything without his permission. But now, at least, I had a purpose in his eyes.

The crimes started small with little tasks like stealing. I knew that my mom and dad stole things all the time because I would watch them. Whenever we went in a store, I would see my mom put things in her purse or my dad stick things down the front of his pants. Sometimes they would have me sit inside the shopping cart baskets with my legs crossed so that they covered the items they hid there. It was different now though because he was teaching me to do it for him, but on my own.

The first time I had to steal for him was absolutely terrifying for me. We were in a grocery store picking up our monthly welfare foods. He pointed to a sling shot and said to put it in my pocket after he left. He then walked out of the store to the car where he waited for us to finish. My mom looked down and told me "Not near me," and so I grabbed it and walked away from her. As I walked down the aisle, I looked around to make sure no one would see me. I put the sling shot in my pocket and continued to walk. I didn't know what to do after it was in my pocket. I wasn't sure if I should go back with my mom or walk out to the car with my dad and so I walked down a few more aisles. I finally decided to go out to the car with my dad.

As I tried to walk through the front doors of the store, a man grabbed my shoulder and told me to come with him. I could feel my heart pounding out of my chest when he said this. I started following him towards a door near the cash registers. My hands and legs were trembling as we walked. He took me into an office where he asked me if I had anything in my pockets. I tried to lie to him, answering "No." He then grabbed my arm and put it on the table in front of me.

"Do you know what they do in the Middle East when a person gets caught stealing?"

"No?"

"They chop the thief's hand off. Do you want us to chop your hand off?"

"No, please, no."

"Then you should be honest with me. Do you have anything in your pockets that is not yours?"

With tears rolling down my cheeks, I reached into my pocket and pulled out the sling shot. He took it from me and placed it on the table in front of me. He told me not to move and then he left the room. A few moments later, he walked back in with my mom. I began sobbing the moment I saw her.

"I'm sorry. I won't do it ever again, I promise. I'm sorry."

The man talked to my mom for a few minutes before she walked me out to the car to leave. As we left the office, the man stopped me one last time.

"Remember what I told you about the Middle East. I hope you never try doing this again."

As we walked out, I could feel every person in the store staring at me in disappointment. I was so embarrassed I kept my head down in shame. When we got to the car, Warner screamed in anger at my mom and me.

"What the f*ck took you guys so long?"

My mom told him what happened. I knew I was going to be beaten for what I had done. I tried to apologize before his anger exploded all over me.

"I'm sorry, I'll never do it again."

He started laughing and told me to "stop."

I was confused. Why was he laughing? Why was he not upset? I had completely forgotten that he told me to steal the sling shot in the first place.

"So, do you still have it? Did you get it for me?"

"No, the man took it from me and said he was going to chop my hand off."

"No he won't" he responded, still laughing. "They are not allowed to touch you. Don't worry, we're gonna learn everything you need to know so that this never happens again."

I was even more confused now. For the rest of the day, he taught me how to steal correctly so that I would never get caught again. He took me to another store where he made me walk in with him over and over, filling my pockets until I had successfully stolen 100 items. He didn't care what they were, as long as I was able to steal from the store. He taught me not to be obvious by looking around before I stole things. He also taught me not to be scared or nervous, as well as how to get away if anyone saw me. He also taught me to notice the reflective windows up on the second floor where the managers could sit and watch me.

"If anyone tries to stop you, do you remember what to do?"

"Yes, scream as loud as I can for my mom and then run away."

"Good! And what if they try to catch you?"

"Run as fast as I can out of the store and don't stop running until I am across the street."

"Good! Remember, they are not allowed to chase you anymore once you are off the store property."

He taught me to walk out the front doors with things in my hands because "when you look like you are doing nothing wrong, no one will ever notice or question you." He taught me all of these tips and tricks with the understanding that if anyone ever asked, my name was Billy, or Michael, or whatever random name that popped into my head. Above all, he made sure I knew to never tell anyone that he taught me or even knew what I was doing.

Stealing became my daily chore in our house. I was ordered to steal under the threats of being beaten. Even with my new purpose, Warner would still take his anger out on me at every chance he had, whether I failed him or not. Sometimes he would give me impossible items to steal just so that he could beat me later for having failed him.

This wasn't his only criminal activity he imparted on me. He started using me to kill animals with him and for him. He was desensitizing and dehumanizing me from a young age to ensure that I would follow his commands without hesitation.

My first introduction to this revulsion was when he took me out to a creek while camping. He brought a box of newborn puppies with us. I didn't understand why he brought them with us until we arrived at the creek. He made me grab the puppies, one at a time from the box and then hold them under the creek water until they drowned. I remember wanting to cry as he made me do this. The puppies were so tiny and innocent, but he made me hold their little black bodies under the freezing creek water until they were dead. Once each one had died, he would have me drop it in the water to float away as he laughed and approved. My hands shook with pain from the freezing cold waters as my heart ached from being forced to commit murder.

This eventually grew into tossing hotdogs with rat poison hidden inside into neighbor's yards. Then it escalated to us catching animals in cages and burning them alive, throwing baby kittens into lakes to die, or dragging them behind his truck by a rope until dead. If I failed at any of Warner's orders, he would immediately beat me for it.

There was one day when he suddenly snapped with anger. I don't remember what he was upset about, but something set him off. I was in the front yard when he came racing around the side of the house on his trike (a three-wheeled motorcycle). He stopped next to the front porch and ran into the front door. He grabbed our pet cat by the back of the neck and stormed back outside the front door. I knew something bad was going to happen and so I quickly moved far away from the house when he stormed in. My mom followed him out the front door crying out, "Warner, Please No!"

He walked over to his truck with the cat in his hand and grabbed out of the truck bed a knotted-up mess of bright yellow twine. He dropped down on his knees so that the cat was stuck, unable to move. He tied the rope around our cat's neck and then jumped up. The cat tried to run away, but he jerked her back with the rope. I intently watched, scared for what was about to happen. I didn't know what he was going to do, but I could see it was something bad. He then tied the other end of the rope to the back of his trike. He looked back at my mom and laughed, "Watch this" as he jumped on the bike and began racing towards the street. I could see my cat suddenly fly into the air when he drove off. My mom called me to come with her into the house.

"Don't watch him. That's what he wants us to do. Just go play in your room quietly so that he doesn't go after you next."

I tried to do as she said and look away, but I couldn't help but to watch him from just inside the front door. He dragged our cat to death, right in front of us. After five or six times racing up and down the road as fast as the three-wheeler would go with the cat dragging behind him, he pulled back into the yard. He grabbed a hammer from his truck and then nailed the cat's dead body to our front door. Before he made it to the front door, I had already run back into my room to hide. I could hear him pounding the nail into the front door while laughing. "Do you like that? Do you see? Next time it will be one of you two mother f*ckers."

We were terrified and knew better than to ever question his authority in any way. Not only because of a fear of the physical abuse, but also the emotional fear that would follow. He often threatened to do to us the same horrors he did to the animals. His words would repeat over and over in my head for days and weeks after. Having been made to torture and kill innocent animals with him, I had an unexplainable fear driven deep into my heart. If he could do these things to animals and laugh about it, who would argue that he wouldn't do the same to us? I started wishing and praying for God to kill me so that Warner couldn't.

I hated my dad, I hated my life, I hated the pain that I was causing everyone else by the mere fact that I was alive.

Forbidden Family Expansions

All throughout the younger years of my childhood, I would create forts deep beneath the house, or under my bed where I would lock myself away for hours at a time. When I was hiding away in my forts, I felt that I was safe and hidden away from being hit, put to work, or having my dad make me stand in front of him while he reminded me that I was a "worthless piece of sh*t." When I was hidden away in my private hiding places, I didn't have to fear my dad forcing me to feel bad about ruining everyone's lives.

I spent most of my childhood playing alone in these forts because I never really had any friends. Anytime I did make friends at school, their parents forbade them to play with me because of my dad's reputation. It seemed that no matter where we were, the people within the community knew all about him and his past criminal records.

During my second-grade year, my parents were arrested for robbing a hospital. While they awaited trial, I was sent to live with my aunt, uncle, and cousin in Morongo Valley, California. In total, I lived with my extended family for four months, while we all awaited the verdict of their trial. I didn't know it at the time, but this move would have a major impact on me for the rest of my life.

Before this time, I was always fearful and felt worthless. I didn't talk much, and I didn't really have any friends. But when I was with them, I felt safe and loved. This family treated me as if I were an actual person with valuable qualities. They encouraged me to speak out and try new things. They believed in me and my potential to succeed. They allowed me to have friends and to talk with them on the phone. They taught me to do my homework and to do "normal kid chores." With all of their love and support, I began to develop self-confidence as well as an interest in the arts.

My life with them had full meals, clean clothes, regular baths, and a warm house at night. Best of all, I was not in constant terror of abuse or death. I began to see myself as a normal kid, whom other people could be friends with. I was not mocked for being dirty, for smelling bad, or for living out of the dumpsters and on Welfare. I was allowed to talk to and have friends at school, and I didn't fear coming home.

One day in school, my teacher read a story to us called One Red Rooster by Kathleen Sullivan Carroll. It was a typical children's story for learning to count. "One red rooster, two cows" etc. After reading the story, my teacher asked us to draw a picture of an animal from the story. At this time, the Teenage Mutant Ninja Turtles were my favorite thing in the world so I, of course, had to draw a turtle. I don't really remember what I thought about while drawing the turtle, but I remember drawing the sun in the sky. At some point before this, I watched my cousin draw a sun with alternating short and long lines or sunbeams coming from the sun. I copied my cousin's alternating lines in my drawing of the turtle. I remember this because I was terrified that I would get in trouble for copying her. I fearfully drew the sunbeams while the teacher was looking away. I wanted to draw my sun just like my cousin drew hers, but I feared that I was going to be in trouble for copying her.

Sometime later, we received a phone call asking us to come to the art fair. I was unaware at the time, but I had won first place for my drawing. When my aunt told me we had to go to the art show for my turtle, I thought for sure this was where they were going catch me for copying. I was so scared that they were going to send me back to live with my parents. I was going to be sent away from my new safe life and forced to live with Warner again. I didn't want to be a bad kid and I didn't want to upset anyone. I was only trying to draw like my cousin did.

Despite these months away from Warner, I was so used to being wrong, bad, and unwanted, that my mind only produced negative possible outcomes. To my surprise, I was not in trouble at all. I remember liking the attention, but I was still afraid of attracting any attention. I was not ever supposed to be seen or heard, and now there were people applauding me and taking my picture. From that day on, I knew art was important to me and that I wanted to be an artist.

After this, every school art project was done with great attention to perfection. Anytime an assignment was given in school that had any artistic attribute, I would put every ounce of care into that project. I would spend my free time engaging in drawing, origami, cross stitch pictures, and other artistic mediums. My teachers and peers often referenced me as "talented" or "gifted." These few months with my aunt, uncle, and cousin changed who I thought I was and that I wasn't worthless at all. In fact, I felt I was considered valuable.

Another exciting outcome that happened during this time, was when I met my maternal grandparents who lived near my aunt, making it possible for me to spend lots of time with them.

One of my favorite memories was going fishing with my grandpa. Whenever he took me fishing, we would have to leave early in the morning before the sun came up. To make it easier to leave on time in the morning, I would stay the night at their house. The night before, I would get to play cards with my grandma and help her feed her dogs. It was so much fun getting to play Go Fish, Speed, Uno, War, and other games.

Then on the morning of our fishing trip, my grandma would wake up early to make us breakfast before we left. We would eat quickly and then jump in the truck with a boat on a trailer behind us. My grandpa was really funny and would make lots of jokes all day long. Then for lunch, he would give me a peanut butter and jelly sandwich and one of his "grumpy grandpa's gourmet cookies."

I also got to meet my paternal grandparents, Warner's parents. They lived about an hour away from my aunt, which made it much harder to spend time with them. Even though I didn't get to see them as often, I remember them as really nice and fun to be with.

When my parents were released from jail, they drove down to my aunt's house to take me back. I was never told why I had to live with my aunt or why I was no longer with my parents, but I had learned to love my new situation. When my aunt told me that my parents were coming to get me again, I thought I was in trouble. I didn't know if I had done something wrong, or maybe my parents heard that I was a good kid and they wanted me now. Part of me was excited as I started to imagine that maybe after this, things were going to be different at home. Maybe we were going to be a normal family. Was it possible that life could or would be wonderful and better? When my parents actually arrived to pick me up, they both seemed so happy. Even my dad was smiling and seemed different. I was so excited to return to them and start living our new lives together.

I quickly learned that I was wrong. They were only pretending in front of people to make themselves look better. Nothing was different. The only thing that changed was that my parents stopped hiding their drug abuse. They would make me hold their drugs for them when we went places. They used to make me look away when I was younger as they snorted lines from their little mirrors right in front of me. Now, Warner would take his syringes and shoot up with me watching, as if it were a totally normal thing to do. I watched him shoot up on his arms, legs, hands, and basically anywhere he could find a vein. When they transitioned from snorting to shooting, my mom began drinking hers. She would mix her drugs into a glass with cola and then drink it.

After picking me up from my aunt's house, my parents decided we were going to stay in southern California. They found us a small triplex apartment in Desert Hot Springs, California. This town was a mostly Hispanic and Black community filled with drugs and crime. It was not an easy place to live as a nine-year-old, white kid with curly red hair. Warner became even more abusive during our time in this city. He began forcing his hatred and racism upon me by making me do and say things to any people of color we came upon. He would make me scream out the "N" word to random strangers, throw rocks at them, spit on them, and say evil things to them.

One day, he had me walk up to a random black woman whom I had never met. My orders were to "Walk up and spit in that n*gger's face." I would rather have died then to do it, but I had no choice with him; I had to do as he instructed. I remember us sitting in his truck waiting for our victim. When he saw a black woman walk out of a convenience store, he nudged me on my arm pushing me towards the truck door.

"That's the b*tch, go show that n*gger".

As I walked down the sidewalk, I could feel my heart pounding through my chest. My legs began to shake, and my throat became dry. The woman could see that I was walking towards her with intent. At first, she looked as though she was going to welcome me, but then she looked behind me and saw my dad. I knew the moment she saw him because she was suddenly struck with a look of panic and fear. She must have seen the fear and pain in my eyes because she did not respond to me when I spit at her. Luckily, my throat was dry and so I really couldn't spit. Reluctantly, I mumbled at the woman.

"Get off of my sidewalk you stupid, f*cking n*gger!"

She immediately stepped down into the parking lot and walked away quickly. I had never felt so dirty or disgusting as I did after being made to treat another human being like that. I avoided looking back at Warner for a moment in fear that he might make me do or say something more. After I knew the woman had enough time to get away, I looked back at my dad in hopes of his approval. I could see he was satisfied and possibly even proud of me for what I had done. For the first time in my life, Warner was beginning to treat me like a part of his family. Even though everything he said was hurtful, he was beginning to talk directly to me and not just about me.

The more I acted like him, the more he seemed to be proud of me.

In third grade, one time, I was walking home from school when a group of teenagers I had never seen before approached me. They asked me if I had any money and then told me I better get some money for them if I wanted to walk that way home again. I tried to ignore them, but they circled around me and started pushing me back and forth. I saw a small gap between two of the boys big enough for me to squeeze through. I ran towards the gap and managed to push my way out of the circle. The whole gang of teenagers started chasing me down the road as I ran for my life. Running home as fast as my little legs would carry me, I could hear voices of the group behind me screaming— "If we ever see you again, we are going to beat you like a red-headed stepchild."

When I got home, I told my mom what happened. I explained that these kids obviously knew who I was because they knew I was a red-headed stepchild. My mom burst into hysterical laughter.

"You think they are stalking you?"

"Yes, obviously. How else would they know?"

"They don't know that you are an actual red-headed stepchild. It's a common saying."

"What is a common saying?"

"I am going to beat you like a red-headed stepchild is a common saying."

By this time, my dad had come into the house with us. When he heard what was going on, he and my mom began laughing uncontrollably about it. This must have been the funniest thing they had ever heard because my dad told me I would never live this down. He said that this joke was going to live forever. He then explained to me that gangs were an issue in that town and that I would not always be safe when out walking.

He told me I needed to be able to protect myself and so he started teaching me how to fight. He started by teaching me basic boxing moves, which scared the life out of me. He would make me fight as hard as I could against him in attempt to hit him. If I ever showed any signs of not giving 100 percent in my attempt, he would hit me back.

"You better learn how to take a hit. It's more important than giving a hit," he instructed.

Later he taught me to start throwing handfuls of rocks at people as I ran towards them to fight. He said that if I could distract them with the rocks long enough to get to them, then I only needed to deliver one good hit up into their neck. One good blow to the Adam's apple would drop them to the ground gasping for air, leaving me open to beat them. He also taught me how to rip the antenna off of a car so that I could use it as a whip, in the event that a person or group were to advance on me.

"One good slap across some n*gger's face with a car antenna will make them all back off."

This was my life for the next couple of years.

Warner was indoctrinating me into his world of hate. I was beginning to fill up with anger and hate at everyone. The worst part about all of this was that it started to work. I was slowly becoming more and more like him every day.

Trailer Trash

I was ten years old when my parents surprised me by coming home with a new baby sister. I wasn't sure what to think during the months leading up to her birth, but Warner seemed excited about her. Warner had another daughter with a different woman years before, but the mother wouldn't allow him to see her. Neither my mom nor dad had ever talked about this girl, making it impossible for me to ever learn anything more about her. During the months of my mom's pregnancy, nothing really changed in terms of daily routines. Mom and dad were still doing drugs, drinking, and smoking, Warner was still beating us, I was still pushed to steal things on a nearly nightly basis, and he was still making us hate anyone who was not "white." But then the day came that they walked in with my sister.

My dad walked into the house with such pride and love in his face.

"Would you like to meet *my* daughter?"

He picked her up from the car seat and tried to show her to me. She began to fuss and cry and so he pulled her away from me and tried to comfort her. The more she continued to cry, the more I could see him changing. He was becoming frustrated and angry. I started to worry. Because I had never seen him with a baby before, I was unsure of how he might react to her crying. Knowing that I could be hit for opening my mouth without permission, I submissively asked him,

"Can I try holding her?"

He reached down and placed her into my arms. Almost immediately, my new little sister stopped crying. It was as if she knew that Warner was a bad person and wanted to get away from him. I looked up at my parents with a little smile of pride. I could see the love in my mom's eyes as she smiled back at me. I didn't do anything special, but my sister stopped crying and seemed to like me. When I looked up at my dad, I could see that I had made a mistake. I could instantly see the anger in his face. His daughter liked me more than him, and now I was going to pay for it.

"Look at this little mommy b*tch! The piece of sh*t has a purpose! Guess what you little f*ggot, now you're a mommy!"

He then turned around and left the house with my mother in tow, leaving my sister and I alone. I don't remember how long they were gone the first time, but once they saw that I could fend for the two of us, they began leaving us for days at a time. A year later, just before 5th grade, they surprised me with a second little sister to take care of.

I had not seen my grandparents on either side since I lived with my aunt three years earlier. But the arrival of my two sisters gave Warner the perfect opportunity to weasel his way back into his parent's lives. He began taking us to visit with my grandparents nearly every day for a few months. During those months, he lied to them about how he was working hard to provide a safe home for his children. He would tell them how the rentals were all too expensive and in unsafe communities.

After months of lies, he somehow managed to convince them to purchase a new home for us. We needed a decent place to live that was in a safe community for the babies. Warner convinced his parents to buy him a piece of property in Morongo Valley, as well as a double wide trailer, and two Subaru cars. They purchased this all with a promise from my dad that he was going to work hard and pay them back. He told them that this was all just a loan so that he could provide a healthy and safe life for his family. Even though my grandparents believed him, I knew he was lying.

My dad sold the first Subaru for drug money a week after we moved into our new home. Almost immediately he started destroying the house. My grandfather passed away a short time after that. I never really had a lot of time with him, and so I don't remember much of him. I just remember every time we went to visit them, my dad would script what I was to say. Anytime I said something out of script, I would pay dearly later when my grandparents couldn't see what was happening.

These scripts would include how great things were at home and how my dad was doing so wonderfully at his job— a job he never had. Often times, he would script out a story for us of how we needed a little extra money for things. He would have me tell a story of how the power blew out and fried our refrigerator. This, of course, always led to my grandmother giving him extra money for a new one. I hated being part of his lies to get their money. It made me feel like a horrible person, but I had no choice.

I can't say for sure, but there were so many times that my grandma would give me a look as if she knew I was lying. It felt as though she knew he was making me tell her the made-up story. Even still, she felt bad for us kids, therefore she would go along with the story and give him the money. Even though these grandparents helped us so much by purchasing a home, vehicles, and giving us money, I was still coerced to try to get more for him. A year later, Warner managed to talk my grandma into buying him a new Dodge Ram pickup truck.

Sadly, after we moved into our new house, it took Warner no time at all to destroy it completely. The windows were painted black from the inside so that no one could see inside. We often had no running water or electricity making the house dark and grim. Dishes would pile up in the sink, while ants, cockroaches, centipedes, and rats would run rampant. Our home was not a place of safe living, but a place of filth and nightmares. The yard was filled with old car parts and garbage. I don't know what started it, but Warner absolutely hated our new neighbors. He would often scream out "here you go fat boy," then throw all of my sisters' dirty diapers out the front door over towards their house. The neighbors seemed like normal and nice people, but for whatever reason, Warner targeted them with his anger. I don't know why the neighbor was called "fat boy," but Warner never really gave a reason for any of his actions.

In retaliation, my neighbors built an eight-foot by four-foot billboard in their front yard. The natural landscape of the front corner of their yard was several feet higher than our yard. This billboard was painted white with huge black spray-painted letters on it, which read—

"My dad's full name" at "our full address", with a huge arrow pointing towards our house, "is a registered child molester."

When this sign was posted, I was so embarrassed and felt dirty and judged. The sign was not about me, but I still felt humiliated and ashamed all the same. I started feeling like people were looking at me and my sisters with pity and disgust. I felt like people looked down on us as if they knew what he was doing to us behind closed doors. The other families in our community forbade their children to be near me. I would occasionally hear people call me "his son" rather than using my name, giving me the feeling that I was expected to act like him. Even though I had slowly grown away from using ASL throughout elementary school, I was still alone and had no voice to call out for help.

This billboard did nothing to slow Warner's anger or actions. He continued to live life as though the billboard didn't exist at all. When he wasn't starting fights with the neighbors, he was doing weird things that only tweakers (drug addicts) would do. The things that only made sense to a person on drugs. There was one morning that we woke up to three telephone poles, fifty-five feet tall, erected in our back yard.

Somehow during the night, this man not only successfully stole three full length telephone poles, but also got them home—by himself. Once he got them home, he dug the holes and cemented them into the ground standing up in our backyard. They were cemented into a perfect triangle with each side being about three feet apart. Along the top, he created a deck so that he could "go up to see when the police were coming."

One of his other "tweaker" ideas manifested when he started boiling the lead sheets from inside of car batteries in our kitchen. He would boil all the lead together in pots and then pour them into coffee cans. They never had a purpose; he just enjoyed doing it.

One night, he was in our kitchen, tearing apart a dirt bike he had stolen. In a fit of rage, he picked up the motor and slammed it into the kitchen floor, creating a hole in the middle of our kitchen. Rather than fixing it, he spray-painted a red circle around the hole as a joke. He would often throw food or diapers at the wall, then tell us to leave it because "the place was disgusting, and we deserved to live in garbage." He started removing strips of carpeting from our living room and then replacing them with random different carpets that he had stolen from other houses.

The house stunk from the filth as it was never cleaned. Because we seldom had running water, any messes that were made were left to rot. At different times throughout my youth, my dad exploded into fits of rage and began throwing objects and hitting my mom and me. As a result of this, there were permanent bloodstains along with food crusted on different walls throughout the house. Our furniture also stunk as it was collected from street corners and or trashcans. The smell of the trashed furniture, unwashed dishes, old stolen carpet, rotting food on the walls, rodent droppings, unflushed toilets, and dirty diapers was enough to make any person sick.

It was even worse when you consider that we lived in the hot desert heat during the day and that these odors were all combined with the smell of our unwashed bodies, dumpster dinner collections, and my parents constant smoking, drinking, and vomiting. I absolutely hated being in that house with them.

I began feeling that the filth of the house was somehow becoming part of me. This caused me to start obsessively cleaning my own room in an attempt not to be part of their horrible lifestyle. I began to fear the filth and started looking for ways to wash myself clean of their filth.

Now that Warner had his own permanent house and had not been locked up in jail for a while, he began getting comfortable. This led to absolute chaos, abuse, crime, and fear in our house. I loved having siblings, but learned quickly that if they were going to live through their childhood with him as a father, I would have to protect them. He had not shown any violent anger towards his daughters yet, but I never knew if or when that might change.

When my dad would start showing signs of becoming outraged, I would quickly take my sisters out on walks. I would load them up into a stroller and take them on three and four-hour long walks around town. As long as they were out of the house, they had a chance of surviving him.

Living like this was an endlessly stressful time for all of us. Although life never seemed as though it would get any better, the birth of my sisters did plant a seed within me—I felt I had a purpose: *to survive*. I became the protector of my two little sisters by making sure they were never close to him when Warner was angry.

Past, Present, Future

My family survived by eating from the dumpsters and free handouts from different churches. We did receive food stamps monthly, but most of those were traded for drugs. We learned the schedule for throwing out perishable foods from different grocery stores, so we would go dig out all of the food thrown away in these dumpsters. The food usually consisted of fried chicken remnants, stale dinner rolls, and half empty cornets of frosting from the bakery section. I hated eating the food from the dumpsters. I felt dirty inside every time we would jump into a dumpster and start collecting food. My clothes often stunk from the filth in the dumpsters, making it impossible for the other kids in school not to tease me.

One time we found nearly 100 "off brand" Oreo cookie packages. This was the only thing we ate for about a month in our house. Each cookie package had a big "x" cut on the front with a razor blade so that they would spill out in the dumpster making them inedible. We collected the cookies off of the dumpster floor and brought all of the packages home. I loved the cookies, but they made my stomach hurt and made my throat burn from having too much sugar. Still, these cookies were better than having nothing at all.

I had a love-hate relationship with school. As much as I hated going to school, it was a welcomed escape from the chaos at home. Being at home was exhausting because I never knew what to expect or what would happen each day. At least at school there was a schedule, free lunch, and no beatings. The kids at school labeled me "dirt ball" and would torment me daily. They all teased, avoided, and hated me for something I had no control over. And I hated them too. I was ashamed and so I never spoke of my family, nor did I ever share any personal opinions in school. I feared that others would know who my dad was, or find out the horrible things I was doing, or the filth in which I lived.

Most of the time, keeping my life a secret was easy, but there were times when the silence actually caused me pain. Because my parents used all of our money on their drugs, we never had food or utilities at home. And because we lived by eating remnants from dumpsters, I would spend many school days with hunger cramps. Lunch was both my favorite and least favorite part of school day. The Welfare program enabled me to receive free lunch at school every day. Even though the other kids would laugh and torment me for being poor and living on Welfare, I loved actually having real food for lunch at school. This was always the most conflicting thirty minutes of my life. During the lunch break, I would see kids eating half their lunch and throwing the rest away. They would mix the vegetables and other foods they didn't want to eat into a pile of slop and then throw it way. I wanted so badly to dig it all out of the trash and take it home for my mom and sisters. But I knew if I did, the students would never let me live it down. Instead, I would sit in silence while I ate every last bite of my own food. As much as I hated school, it was still my favorite part of the week. It made me feel poor, disgusting, dirty, unlikeable, and pathetic, but it was better than being at home with my monster of a father and most certainly better than starving. During the weekends, I would often not get to eat at all.

I was eleven years old during the summer break between fifth and sixth grade. I had been out pulling weeds for my dad all morning. I started walking towards the house to get a drink of water. As I approached the back door of the house, the sound of conversations and laughter filled the air. I instantly felt like this was a safe day because my dad was in a good mood. I began walking up the five stubby brick stairs towards the door. Just as I reached out to grab the doorknob, the back door suddenly opened before I could get there. Warner was standing in the doorway peering down at me.

"What do you want? Why are you here?"

I was instantly caught off guard and became scared. I looked down, making sure not to make eye contact with him.

"May I get some water please?"

As these words left my mouth, I could sense him peering out over me into the yard to evaluate my progress.

"Why is my bike moved? Did you touch my bike you worthless little n*gger?"

"Yes." I cautiously answered while trying to back away slowly down the stairs. "I needed to move it so I could get to the weeds behind it."

Without warning, I felt a sudden force slam across the side of my face. The impact was so fierce that it caused me to fly off the steps, slamming hard into the concrete. Up until this point, he had never hit me with such a force. It happened so quickly that I couldn't comprehend what had just happened. I was frantically filled with such a sudden fear that I didn't know what to do. I didn't know if I should lay there motionless, run, or try to apologize. Slowly, I raised up onto my knees and lowered my head, looking at his feet to acknowledge my mistake. I should have known better; I shouldn't have touched his possessions. After everything stopped spinning and I'd managed to catch my breath, I stood up, still looking obediently to the ground. My knees were shaking, and my heart was pounding. I knew better than to look at him, speak, or cry as he could see all of these as some kind of challenge to his power. And to challenge him was to be hit again.

He stomped down the steps into the backyard. "Follow me, I have a job for you. And don't come near my house until you are finished."

He grabbed a shovel that was leaning against the garage next to where I was standing. My heart leapt and I shuttered as he quickly reached out to grab it. I thought he was coming at me to hit me again. He walked to the edge of the concrete patio and slammed the shovel into to ground.

"You are going to start digging here."

He then started walking out into the backyard marking a line in the dirt by dragging the shovel behind him.

"I want this trench to be one foot wide and eighteen inches deep." I could feel my eyes welling up with tears as he continued to walk for what felt like a mile. In total, the trench was about seventy feet long.

I knew he would measure every inch to make sure I followed his instructions exactly. If I was unable to meet his demands, I would be beaten for disobeying him. The property was large and filled with gravel and large rocks, making the digging process difficult. I worked as long as I could before nightfall came when I fell asleep in the yard. I don't remember the time, or even lying down for that matter. I do remember waking up the next morning in fear that he would catch me sleeping. I immediately jumped up and continued the job assigned to me.

As I worked relentlessly, my back began to ache. I stopped for a breath of air and to stretch my back from being hunched over digging. As I stood there trying to relieve the pain for a moment, he suddenly appeared screaming from across the yard that I was a fat, lazy piece of crap. Struck with shock and fear of his sudden appearance, I immediately began digging again in hopes that he would leave me alone. He continued ranting for what felt like hours.

"You are just like your mother. You are nothing more than another fat, piece of sh*t! I can't stand to even look at you. You make me sick. Get the f*ck out of here you worthless little n*gger lover!"

I tried to continue digging.

"No, you're done, get the f*ck out of here or I'll beat you like a red-headed stepchild, GO!"

I was terrified of what he would do next, so I left. I ran into the desert where he would not be able to find me and then followed the wash for several miles until I was at the highway.

I hitch-hiked my way to my maternal grandparent's house in the neighboring town. Warner had cut off all ties to my mom's parents after second grade when I lived with my aunt. Even after not seeing them for nearly four years, I still remembered how to get to their house. Since I was not allowed to ever see them, I figured he wouldn't think to look for me there if he changed his mind and wanted me to return home.

When I got there, my grandmother told me to take a shower while she washed my clothes. I had nothing to wear while they were in the washer and so she gave me one of her oversized sweatshirts to wear. I was still small enough that the adult sized shirt hung all the way down to my knees like a night gown. I don't know how my parents knew where I was, but during the short time that my clothes were in the washer, my mom showed up with my sisters and his orders to bring me home to finish the trench. My heart sank when I saw her because I knew I was going to have to go back.

My mom tried to comfort me the whole drive home. She apologized and told me everything would be fine if I just finished the trench. She tried justifying his actions, but we both knew there were no justifications. She told me if I worked fast enough to finish the trench, he would let me go to my room and then it would all be over. Despite her attempt to comfort me, my imagination was filled with horrible terrors and fears of what was waiting for me when I got home. As we pulled into our driveway, I could see my dad in the front yard waiting.

Because my clothes were still in the washer when my mom picked me up, I had to wear the oversized sweatshirt home. As I stepped out of the vehicle, he began laughing at me for wearing the oversized sweatshirt. He said that it looked like I was wearing a dress, and that I had finally switched over to a woman. I was used to him calling me names and telling me I was worthless, but this was the start of a new name-calling. This day was a turning point. I was no longer the worthless, hated, piece of sh*t—like before. This was the start of a whole new sexualized form of abuse.

From that day forward, he began referring to me as "the f*ggot." He rarely used my name before this, but now he stopped using my name completely. He would call me any negative comment that came to his mind at the given moment.

Sometimes this was "c*cksucker," other times it was "n*gger lover." It changed day by day but was usually based around a homosexual orientation. He also began giving me different jobs inside the house that he would refer to as "woman's work," or "b*tch jobs." These were often times simple cleaning jobs, but he would use these as his time to torment me with this new, sexual form of emotional abuse. Every job he concocted was used as a way to demoralize me. He would make me scrub the floor so that I could spend "additional time on your knees." He would make fun of me while I scrubbed the floors telling me that I "enjoyed it on my knees."

After this, I stopped talking to any and all boys at school because I was terrified that he would accuse me of being gay and then beat me for it. Part of me also feared that if he did ever find any excuse to label me as "gay," then the abuse might become even worse.

He would say weird things that always made me feel terribly uncomfortable and fearful. "I'd rather hear a fat boy fart than a pretty girl sing," and "there's not much better in the world than a young boy's tight little *sshole." There many were times he would torment me with his ridicule.

"I want you to get in the kitchen and scrub the floor. It had better be spotless too; you're going to be eating off of it tonight."

As I sat on my knees scrubbing with all my might, I could feel him walking up behind me. I knew better than to turn and look.

"Hey, you little f*ggot. You wanna suck my d*ck?"

I could hear him unzipping his pants just inches behind my head.

"Are you ready? You're working pretty hard in here; you must be ready for a little reward."

I knew better than to stop working or to acknowledge him being there. I continued to scrub with all my might, pretending that I did not know he was there. He would burst out laughing at me:

"You little f*ggot b*tch. I know you want to suck my d*ck."

Sometimes he would continue this for hours, laughing at me as he accused me of "looking forward to it and being excited to do it." I never had to actually perform sexual acts, nor did I ever see any parts of his body, but there was always that fear that he would snap at any moment actually making me do something sexual for him.

Shots Fired

On Thanksgiving Day of sixth grade, my dad was behaving even worse than he did normally. I don't know what had originally set him off, but he was going to punish us all for it. I was trying to keep my sisters as far away from him as possible by keeping them with me in their bedroom. Every room in the house was connected to the living room of our little nine hundred square foot mobile home. This made it difficult to keep my sisters more than a few yards away from their dad.

Warner brought a metal trash can into the living room where he was burning things in the house. He was throwing anything he could grab from in the house into the fire. The front door was closed, causing the living room to fill up with smoke. He grabbed something that was made of fabric to throw into the fire. My mother suddenly screamed out at him.

"Wait, please don't burn that. It belongs to my mother and is irreplaceable. Let me call her to come get it."

He threw it back onto the floor and left the room. She picked up the phone to call her mom to come get the item. A few moments later, he walked into the room and saw her on the phone. I could see it in his entire body when he saw her, that he had suddenly snapped. He ran over to her and ripped the phone cord out of the wall. He wrapped the phone cord around her neck and dragged her through the house into the kitchen. My sisters were screaming and crying as our mom was being dragged across the floor. Her face was red as she gasped for air while kicking and scratching to get free.

He grabbed my mom up off the floor and threw her face down onto the kitchen table. He grabbed her by the hair, pressing her face into the table, and put a knife to her throat. At that point, he stopped and stared at me to see what my response would be. I knew that if I panicked, said a word, or showed any fear, he would have slit her throat and then come after me and my sisters. I knew at that moment he was not only willing— but ready to kill us all. I tried to calm him down by doing what he wanted. I looked down to the floor and tried to walk away hoping that my submission to him would get him to stop. Angrily, he screamed across the house,

"Do something you little f*ggot! Be a man, do something!"

I looked up at him in absolute terror and astonishment before I looked back down at the floor. I lowered my head as I looked down to show him that he was in control and none of us would ever question that.

I wished so badly that the police would come bursting through the door to stop him. I wished that he would lose interest and just leave. *I wished he would suddenly overdose on meth and drop dead.* But none of those things happened. None of these options were a possibility for us because any rescue just simply wasn't a reality in our lives.

He quickly dragged the knife through the side of my mother's neck, threw her to the floor and told us that next time he would kill her. He walked back over to the trashcan and continued burning stuff. I tried to calm my sisters down so that he would not turn on them for crying. My mom continued to lay on the floor holding her neck and crying. He started throwing larger items out into the front yard. With each item he threw out the front door or burned in the trash can, he would look at us for a response. He was trying to get us to react to his actions so that he would have an excuse to kill us.

This continued on for what felt like an eternity. Suddenly, we all heard a loud noise come from just outside our front door. It sounded like a car had just crashed onto our property. I opened the front door a tiny crack to see what the sound was. When I peeked out, I saw my grandfather standing at the bottom of our five small steps. I was surprised to see him standing there, as I had not seen him since the sweatshirt incident. My dad heard my surprised voice when I saw him.

"Grandpa?"

Warner quickly ran to the front door slamming me to the side and out of his way. My grandpa pointed a gun at my dad's face. Warner picked up the older of my two sisters and held her in front of him as he began antagonizing my grandfather. She couldn't fight to get away as she was barley under three years old. Warner hugged her close to his chest as he hid behind her.

"Do it p*ssy, let's see you do it. Be a big man and shoot me. You don't have the balls."

My grandfather didn't move a muscle as he calmly replied,

"You be a man. Put down the baby and find out."

Warner put my sister down, then suddenly flew against the back wall. I was painted with Warner's blood as the sound of the gun rang out. I looked back at him on the floor when I realized that my grandpa had done it—he shot my dad. Both of my sisters were screaming as my mom and I looked at Warner on the floor.

Warner put his hand up onto his face where he was shot, then stood up in anger. His face was pouring blood as he ran to the front door while screaming at my grandpa.

"You're dead motherf*cker!"

He bolted out the front door, chasing my grandfather down the street. I stood there for a moment in absolute shock of what just happened before my mom in a tone of total disappointment turned to me.

"Will you go call 911 from the neighbor's house?"

My dad and grandpa ran so fast that I could no longer see either of them. I walked next door and rang the doorbell of my neighbor's house. I could see the absolute shock in her eyes as she opened the door.

"Oh my God, are you ok?"

"Yes, we are all fine. This is all Warner's blood."

"Wait, is he dead?" She asked, as a glimmer of hope seemed to creep out from the corners of her slightly smirking smile.

"No, my grandpa shot him in the face, but he got up and started chasing him. I think he is going to kill my grandpa."

We called the police, but they seemed more worried about my grandfather's safety than Warner's life. My dad came home a short while later after he realized he couldn't catch my grandpa. He lay in the middle of our living room floor, bleeding out while we waited for the paramedics. Although on one hand, we were all scared for my dad, I know that my mom and I both secretly hoped he would die. It took the paramedics an especially long time to bring an ambulance down to our house for Warner. Our little town was a forty-five-minute drive away from the nearest hospital. We only had one road into town and one road out. On this night, the ambulance took well over an hour and a half to get to Warner.

Somehow, my dad lived through this whole mess, only to come out of the hospital with a new scar. He openly bragged that the doctors were shocked he could live through such an event. They told him that if the bullet had entered his face a millimeter in any other direction from where it was, he would have died.

Our entire valley community knew who my dad was and hated him. When my grandfather stood before the judge for attempted murder, the judge didn't even try to hide his bias. My grandpa was retired from the Navy (with a very high ranking) and had a Conceal Carry Weapon license. He was an honored and respected man in his community and so the judge had already formed a bias in my grandpa's favor.

"How did you not kill him? How did you manage to shoot him in the face and not kill him?" The judge asked.

He sentenced my grandpa to four hundred hours of community service helping to keep Big Bear Lake clean. The judge knew that my grandpa enjoyed fishing, so he figured this seemed a worthy punishment. He also strongly recommended that my grandpa go practice in the shooting ranges some more; so that if there were ever a next time, they wouldn't be having the same conversation.

A few days after being shot, Warner was released from the hospital. When he came home, he was somehow different. He now believed that he was invincible. He started trying to make us worship him. He turned everything into a joke about him being a "god," but he wouldn't say the word "god." He would do it in a British accent as if he were a knight at the king's table and pronounce it "Gwad."

"I have been chosen by Gwad to be here. Gwad made me as the perfect person to help cleanse his planet. Gwad wants me to clean the Earth of all you vermin n*ggers. I am now your new Gwad."

During his first week home from the hospital as "Gwad," a young man from up the street stopped by with bins of food. He told us that he had thrown a Thanksgiving party and had lots of food left over. Because he was a bachelor, the food would have gone to waste. Rather than throwing it all out, he offered it to us. Because my family seldom had food in the house, this was a big deal for us. We graciously accepted this wonderful gift. Little did I know at the time; this man would have a lasting impact on my future.

Freezing Nights & Rotting Flesh

Several weeks later, just before Christmas day, I heard the roar of fire truck sirens ringing throughout our house. My heart sank as the sirens became louder and closer. I could see the colored lights flashing through the house. I knew for sure something was wrong, and they were coming for us. My parents were gone, leaving only my sisters and me at home alone. My heart pounded and my knees shook. I knew there was no point in running, so I opened the front door in hopes that they were going to a neighbor's house. They pulled up to the front of the house and stopped. I could feel my legs shaking as fear started to take over my body. I could feel my face turning red as I tried not to pass out from fear.

To my surprise, Santa Claus jumped out of the fire truck and started walking towards me. I could see the neighbors all standing on their front porches watching what was happening.

I was both embarrassed and confused as Santa Claus walked up to my front door with a big bag slung over his shoulder. He reached his hand out to hand me the bag. I looked out at all the neighbors in their front doors staring at me. It felt like I was doing something wrong. I tried to decline him by shaking my hand "no" at him, but he smiled reassuringly at me that everything was alright.

"It's ok, they are for your family. Merry Christmas."

I hesitantly took the bag from him and said, "thank you." He smiled and began to walk back to the truck.

After Santa and the firetruck pulled away, I shut the front door and put the whole bag next to my parents' bedroom door. I peeked into the bag to see what was inside. The bag was full of beautifully wrapped Christmas gifts. I knew better than to open anything in the bag without Warner's permission. Consequently, I never got to see anything more than the little peek I took into the top of the bag. When my parents got home, I told them what had happened. My dad took the bag and tossed it into the corner of our living room. When I woke up in the morning, the gifts were gone. I knew better than to ask about them, as questioning him resulted in being beaten. My dad had sold them, traded them, or simply threw them away. We were not deserving of Christmas gifts in the eyes of my father.

After Christmas break that year, my school had a fundraiser where students could sell pizzas. I don't remember what the prize was for the top seller, but I knew that I wanted it. I began selling pizzas as if my life depended on it. I took my sisters with me and knocked on every door in my town. When the people answered their doors, I basically begged them to buy a pizza from me for the fund raiser. By the end of the first week, I had sold nearly $1,000 worth of pizzas. I was determined to prove my worth, and to prove that I could do great things. The fundraiser was set up so that students would collect and turn in the money. Then two weeks later, the same students would deliver the pizzas to the people who had purchased them. As I sold the pizzas, I knew better than to let my dad see the money I collected. If he saw that I had money, I was certain that he would steal it from me.

My bedroom had two vents in the floor for our non-existent furnace. Seeing as there was no heat coming from the vents, I took the two screws out of one of the grates covering the vents and hid the money down under the floor. I put the money in an envelope and then put a rubber band around the envelope and slid it as far as my arm would reach down. Every night after I added more money from new sales, I would screw the grate back down over the vent. The night before I was supposed to turn in the money for the pizzas, I reached into the vent to grab my envelope. When I pulled it out, my rubber band was still on it, but every dollar was gone. My dad had found it and stolen every last dollar.

I don't remember what I told the school, but I knew I was in a lot of trouble. My dad accused me of being irresponsible for losing the money. I knew better than to tell anyone what really happened. If I accused him of stealing the money from me, I would have been beaten like never before. As embarrassed as I was, I had to go along with his story that I had lost all the money. Because I was so young, I could not be held accountable to pay back the money. Instead, I was heavily punished by the school. They gave me detention and banned me from participating in any future fundraisers. Everyone was so ashamed of me. I had let my imagination get the best of me by thinking that perhaps I could show the world that I had any value. I thought I could earn forgiveness and acceptance if I sold enough pizzas. But I was wrong and was only reminded that people like me were not deserving.

Winters in the desert are misleading, especially at night. By all means, it does not snow or feel like what most people would say is cold. However, for us who are used to the desert heat, winters were cold, especially at night. Our mobile home was always cold, and we seldom had propane or electricity for heat. The cold winds would blow in through our open swamp cooler, our broken windows, through the hole in the kitchen from under the house, and through the open cracks around the windows.

Sometimes, we would find or steal a five-gallon propane tank to warm the house a little. My dad had a roofer's blow torch attachment that he would attach to the propane tank. It was a long stick with a hose on one side to attach to the tank and a trigger on the other. We would turn the tank on and then light the blow torch side so that a giant flame would roar out into the air. We would use this blow torch to make a few passes through the house to help warm us all up a little. It smelled horrible, but it was better than freezing. If we ever did have electricity, my sisters and I would have burn marks where our veins would surface against our skin after we fell asleep snuggling up against the heater.

Most nights, my sisters and I would curl up under blankets, then throw dirty laundry on top of us. Then we would put our heads under the blanket with a small tunnel for our noses to breathe in fresh air. We would breathe in through our noses and then out of our mouths under the blanket to help warm up our bodies. We didn't have any pajamas so we would sleep in our jeans and shirts that we wore throughout the day.

We all found our own way of staying warm despite the winter's chill. Mom and dad used the added kick of drugs for their warmth, while we kids huddled together. I discovered that putting my dirty socks and shoes on in the morning physically hurt my feet. My socks would dry out from the sweat and dirt and become crunchy and hard. Then my shoes would press the hard-crunchy socks against my feet causing me pain until they softened up again. To avoid this, I stopped taking my socks and shoes off at night. Not only did this help to avoid the discomfort, but it also helped to keep my feet warm at night.

One day during an after-school practice for a school event, my sixth-grade teacher wanted us to trace the silhouette of our bodies on paper. She had the floor covered in a special giant sheet of paper for us to lay down on but needed us to walk across it to lay in our places. To help avoid us accidentally ripping or marking the paper with our shoes, she gave us the instructions:

"Ok, class. Everyone, take off your shoes and carefully find a place on the paper."

My heart pounded as I heard her say these words. I quietly walked over to the teacher and asked her, "Can I please keep my shoes on?"

"No, I need all of you to have your shoes off for this part."

"I can't take my shoes off. I am not allowed."

"I don't want to argue about this right now. You will be fine. Now take them off and find your place on the paper."

Reluctantly, I did as I was told. As I took my shoes off, I could feel the other students staring at me as they began to laugh and make fun of me. I could see the distress on my teacher's face as I removed my shoes. My socks were nearly black with filth, they had holes in them, and the stench was awful. The murmurs and taunting grew as the teacher tried to regain control of her class.

Ashamed, I grabbed my shoes and ran out of class. The smell and sight of my feet was even appalling to me, and now my classmates all knew. I walked home crying as I thought about all the hurtful things my peers said to me. I decided I would never take my shoes off again in hopes that this would be forgotten.

The school reached out to my mom about what was seen that day. She asked me to take my shoes off for her to see. She was horrified as we tried to peel the socks from the skin on my feet. My feet had rotted so badly that my toenails were peeling off. The smell of rotting flesh was so thick that my mom was gasping for clean air.

My mom selected a few foot medications for me to steal the next time we were out shoplifting for my dad. She had me steal a cream to rub on my feet, a powder to put in my shoes before I put them on, and a spray to spray in my shoes after taking them off. She also had me steal a package of socks and a new pair of shoes before making me promise to change my socks every day. As embarrassing as it was, I can't help but wonder how much longer I would have had before developing gangrene and eventually dying.

As hard as it is to believe, that horrifying day may have saved my life.

Fires

My dad pretended that nothing bad had even happened. My feet were not his concern and so things continued on exactly the same as always for him. My feet had not even had enough time to heal before he had me back out committing crimes with him.

One night my dad took me with him to a neighboring town. I remember being filled with fear and anticipation as we drove down the long, dark, dirt road. Every muscle was clenched, and my heart pounded as we raced down the road in his truck. He didn't want anyone to see us driving out there, so he drove without the headlights, relying only on the moonlight to guide us.

We finally slowed to a stop in the middle of what appeared to be a junkyard out in the middle of nowhere. As I looked a little closer, I could see a little trailer home towards the back. We quickly jumped out of the truck and broke into the trailer through the front door. I followed my dad to a small room in the back. It was dark and cluttered, so I trailed closely behind him. In the back room, my dad opened a small hidden door in the floor. We quickly climbed down the ladder into a hidden basement.

Warner began handing me different things to take out to the truck. In a matter of minutes, we had cleared this room of huge guns and boxes of ammunition. We also grabbed several boxes filled with drug paraphernalia. With the last couple of boxes in our hands, my dad grabbed a gas can from the truck and began pouring gasoline all over the floor and walls of the hidden basement. He continued this up the ladder and up into the actual home. Before we left, he lit the house on fire before we raced off in the truck.

After flying back down the moonlit dirt road, we drove out to a hill so that we could sit and watch the fire as the house burned down. As we sat and watched from a distance, we could see huge explosions coming from the house and other secret rooms we did not find underground. I don't know to whom it all belonged, or why we burned the place down, but I remember my dad laughing hysterically as the police, firemen, and helicopters searched the area. As the trailer burned, the things inside caused massive explosions. My dad called it "our own little personal 4th of July party."

The act of breaking in, robbing, and then burning down the remains became a common practice for us. Anytime someone would upset my dad in some way, he would seek revenge by doing horrible things to the person and their family. Some of these retaliations included breaking windows, slashing tires, killing pets, robbery, physical violence, arson, vandalism, and leaving the residents of these places with terrifying fear in their lives. He would regularly have me feed hotdogs filled with rat poison to the animals of people he did not like. I learned from a young age that there were ways a person could seek revenge on others without ever getting caught.

With all the anger and pain bottled up inside me, I had begun to use the skills Warner taught me to blend in flawlessly with my own delinquent groups of peers at school. Unintentionally, I was quickly becoming a horrible little monster at school. I began doing horrible things to people at school as a way to "impress" others.

If there was anything I could do to earn acceptance at school amongst my peers, I would do it. I don't remember why, but some friends and I decided to break into a house early one morning on the way to school. After getting into the house, we destroyed the insides by kicking holes in the walls, throwing things, and breaking anything possible. When we were finished, mimicking the acts of my father, we lit the house on fire and ran away. As it turned out, someone had seen us breaking into the house and had already called the police. Although I did get arrested and sentenced to a sizeable amount of community service hours, my dad was only upset by the fact that I was caught.

The more I acted like him, the less he would target me with his hate and anger. When his anger was no longer directed at me, he would then turn all of it towards my mom. He began making me join in with him, targeting her. He would have me yell things at my mother and treat her as he did. If he was in a moment of rage, he would tell me to call my mother a "worthless fat b*tch." I knew that if I did not do as he commanded, he would turn on me, and then my mother. Then we would both be the victims of that day's rage. I absolutely hated doing it, but I would scream his words at my mother while she sat on the couch looking down at the floor.

I loved my mom, but she made sure I knew to always do as he told me without question, even when that meant hurting her. I could see the pain in her eyes when he made me call her names, make fun of her, throw things at her, and treat her like he did. It hurt so deep inside to do these things to my own mother, but we both knew I had to do it to survive.

In his house, I learned very quickly the differences between physical and emotional abuse. When he was physically abusive, he would hit my mother and me, throw things at us, kick us, or hit us with objects. The physical abuse was often a surprise to me, as I never really knew when it was coming. He would be in a happy mood and then suddenly switch in the blink of an eye to an angry, out of control, abusive monster. His abuse would come and go without warning and, much like his temper, the pain would quickly come and go with it as well. After years of being treated this way, it was easy to become emotionally calloused. I learned that physical pain only lasted a short amount of time and that when he was done hitting me, the pain would slowly begin to fade.

The emotional abuse however, his promises and threats of impending pain, were tormenting. His threats of violence, death, starvation, incarceration, public humiliation, homelessness, and/or sexual acts would strike fear and pain into my every thought. I would sit and think about what he said or what he was going to do to my mom, sisters, or me. These threats would take over my every thought, causing me to lose sight of reality.

I began dreaming about killing him. My hatred began to grow to the point that I began imagining myself killing him. I could no longer wish for my own death as I knew my sisters needed me now. If I was finally freed of this horrible life, my sisters would be stuck living through the same horrible fate I had been subjected to. Bizarrely, I felt my only way to freedom was to kill Warner.

Life continued on this way for as long as I can remember. At the start of each month, my mom would get a welfare check. Once the check came in, my parents would disappear for a few days at a time. I would have no idea where they were. Whenever they did come home, I would take my sisters away from the house for hours at a time. The more time we spent away from Warner, the less pain we would have to endure.

Even though he never hit my sisters, there was always a fear that someday he might.

We never knew what to expect when in his house, but when we were out walking around and away from him, we felt a little more in control of our own safety. Most of the time, we would simply walk for hours up and down the streets, all over the sad-looking town.

Shelter from the Storm

My mom was a sweet and loving person who only wanted the best for her children, but Warner made that impossible for her. After years of being with him, she started showing traits of having possibly developed "learned helplessness." She felt that she not only needed Warner, but also that she deserved every horrible thing that happened to her. Consequently, she never questioned him or tried to stop his actions. I know it hurt her to see how he treated me, but she couldn't stop him.

There were times that Warner would leave by himself, leaving my mom and us kids home alone. My mom would somehow get the strength and courage to try and escape. She would whisper to me that we were going to run away somewhere he would never find us. She would tell me to quickly grab a few pairs of clothes for my sisters and myself and maybe one small toy for each girl. We would both grab a few things from the house and then leave. We often had to run away on foot because Warner usually had all of the car keys with him. Sometimes we would get lucky and be able to take a car, but that was rare. Most of our escapes consisted of us walking down the road with dreams of freedom or asking a neighbor for a ride.

My mom's weight and size made walking really difficult for her. Whenever we tried to run away, I would carry a plastic milkcrate with us for her to sit and rest on. My mom would push my sisters in a stroller so that she could use the stroller to help stabilize her. I would drag a wagon filled with the milkcrate and our possessions alongside her. We would stop for a moment of rest every four to five minutes for my mom. I could see that she was in physical pain, but her determination to break free of Warner was greater than the pain. Most of the time, we would end up in abuse shelters.

I hated the abuse shelters. As much as I hated being around my dad, it was better than being in the abuse shelters. These places felt like prison for everyone inside. The people in charge would put us into a small bedroom with only one bed and then take away all of our stuff. These "safe houses" were really small, meaning there was no room to move around or play. If we were lucky, my sisters would get a play pen to play in. Otherwise, we would have to hold them so that they didn't crawl anywhere. My mom would have to go to "special classes" while I would have to sit and do puzzles. Children were never allowed outside the house, and they had no video games or anything else to do.

To occupy my time, I would sit for hours doing puzzle after puzzle that were available for kids. I knew my mom would cry a lot because she would come back from her classes with her eyes all red and puffy. We were not allowed to leave the house for any reason what-so-ever. I wasn't even allowed to go to school. When we went into these places, there was a required length of time for us to stay. It was usually two weeks; sometimes longer. For that entire length of time, we were not allowed to have any contact with the outside world.

By the end of the required time, my mom usually started to build up confidence. No matter how strong she felt, I knew it was all just false hopes and dreams. No matter how determined my mom was, she would *always* go back to my dad. She would always give in and take us all back to my dad a day or two after leaving the safe house. I never understood why she did this. We would run away, and start to pull our lives together, but then she would go talk to my dad. He would apologize, make empty promises of a better life, and then we would go home again. We all knew he was lying, but we would always go back anyway.

Teenage Death Wishes

Warner never stopped his consistent emotional and physical abuse. Some days were better than others, but the best days were the start of every month. When the welfare check came in, my parents would get their drugs and then life was good for us for a week. We would go dumpster diving for food in the grocery store dumpsters twice a week, visit a local church on Sunday for free bread to take home, and do some shoplifting "runs" throughout the week. I started stealing bottles of alcohol for my dad that I would save for when he started to get angry. Knowing that he was a "happy drunk," I would save these bottles for the days when he started "coming down" from his drugs.

As I prepared to move into middle school, I knew this would be a good time to start earning points with Warner. When it came to picking elective classes in junior high, I picked auto mechanics and Spanish so that he would see that I was not a "worthless f*ggot." Still, I remember his look of disapproval as I climbed into his truck after course selections.

"What bullsh*t schedule did you pick? A bunch of f*ggot classes; cooking and sewing?"

I proudly showed him my course selection paper.

"No, I am really excited; I chose auto mechanics and Spanish. The counselor said that if I take auto for both years of Junior High, then I can take the high school auto class at the community college when I get to high school."

To my surprise, my plan actually worked. For the rest of that week there was no hitting, and no horrible mental games where he would sit and make fun of me. After I selected the courses that I knew he would approve of, he treated me as if he actually approved of me. He even began asking me to help him when he worked on his truck and stolen dirt bikes. I picked the auto and Spanish classes because he had learned a bit of Spanish throughout his life and because he had gone to auto school for a short time after his release in Susanville when I was six.

I never shared it with anyone, but I wanted so badly to take the arts pathway. For the arts pathway, students would spend a trimester in culinary, art, and music. I loved art, and had always wanted to play music, but was never allowed.

During my 6th grade year, a teacher came to our school to teach us music. After being introduced to the options, we all got to pick an instrument to learn. The teacher had to do a lotto style name choosing after nearly all of the boys chose drums. I was not one of the lucky chosen few. I tried for trumpet, then clarinet, but got neither. In the end, the only instrument left was the flute. I didn't care because I was excited to play anything they would let me. I remembered that my cousin played the flute, but I didn't care if it was a girly instrument. When I came home and told my parents, Warner freaked out.

"You d*ck-sucking little f*ggot. You think you are going to play the flute? Not in this house! The only flute you'll play is my skin flute!"

Needless to say, I decided not to learn an instrument that year. Remembering how he reacted in 6th grade about music, I knew better than to sign up for the arts electives in middle school. I knew my safest option was to pick the classes he would approve of.

Victims & Monsters

I was now in seventh grade and my sisters were two and three years old. One day, my dad randomly brought home a dog for us to have as a family pet. I loved putting my sisters into a little red wagon and then taking them out to walk the dog. I started using "walking the dog" as an excuse to get me and my sisters out of the house. About a month after getting our dog, I took my sisters and the dog on a walk down to the local Circle-K convenient store. When we got there, a man we had never seen before angrily walked up to us.

"Your Red Dog's kids, aren't you?"

(Because of his long red beard, Red Dog was Warner's street name.) I had been trained not to talk to anyone and so I signed back to the man in ASL.

"Sorry, I am deaf."

The man burst out laughing. I began to wonder if this was a test.

"Yeah, you are for sure Red Dog's Kid. He has trained you well. Where is your dad?"

I realized in that moment that this was not a test. I knew intuitively and immediately something bad was about to happen. I grabbed my sisters and quickly left the Circle-K to get home. As we started to leave, we noticed the man following us in his little red pickup truck. I didn't know who he was or what he was going to do to us, so I picked up my sisters and ran into the desert where he could not follow us in his truck. We could see the guy going up and down the streets looking for us in the deserts. Our house was about two miles from the Circle-K making it impossible not to cross several streets while running from one desert to another. While in the deserts, we would hide behind bushes and walk in the washes so he wouldn't see us. We knew all of the trails and places to hide from the times we ran from Warner.

We would sneak up to the edge of one desert, peeking out from the bushes onto the street to make sure the man in the red pick-up truck wouldn't see us when we ran across. Then we would run across the street as fast as we could into another desert before ducking down behind more bushes. We managed to remain unseen by the man all the way up to our street. Because there were no deserts that connected to our house, I knew we would eventually have to walk exposed down our home street. After taking a final look from behind the bushes for the man, we started walking as quickly as my sisters could handle down our street. We thought we were safe as we had not seen his truck in in a while.

As we got within a few houses from home, the man came driving down my street. He jumped out of the truck and began screaming at us in a complete rage.

"Where is your dad? Where is Red Dog?"

I began to sign to him when he screamed again.

"I am not stupid; I know you can speak."

Before I could say a word, the man ran into my house looking for my dad. No one was home, which only upset him more. When he came out, he ran down our driveway towards my sisters and me. As he approached us, our dog began to growl and bark at him, protecting us. I started to back away with my sisters. The man stopped and stared at us for a moment, then pulled out a gun and shot my dog.

"Tell your dad I stopped by and that I'll see him later."

Then he jumped in his truck and drove away.

My sisters were crying hysterically. I quickly took them into the house to help calm them down. Even though we only had our dog for about a month total, it still broke our hearts to lose him. It seemed like nothing good could ever last in our lives.

I don't remember how my dad reacted to me telling him what happened, nor do I remember what he did about it. I just remember always being afraid that the man was going to come back and kill us all.

As time passed, Warner began making me carry out more criminal activities with him. He would take me to stores with "shopping lists" of items to steal for him nearly every day. He would drop me off at a store and tell me to come back with his items. Sometimes these "lists" would be only one or two items, while other times it would be an entire cart worth. It was my job to figure out how to steal what he wanted. After I got everything he wanted, I would start walking down the street away from the store. He would be waiting somewhere up the road in his truck. Once he saw that I was a safe distance away from the store, he would drive over to pick me up.

Warner also started taking me to rob houses with him. He would drive us out to an area near the house we were going to steal from. He would find some random place a few blocks away to park the truck before walking to the target house. We would do this in the middle of the day as a means of "not attracting attention." We would walk straight up into the house's backyard where we were no longer visible by the neighbors. As long as we walked normally, no one ever paid any attention to us. When we acted like we were doing nothing wrong, nobody assumed we were there out of the ordinary.

Once hidden in the back yard, we would find a way into the house. Our usual means of getting in was by shimmying a window open. If we pressed our palms up against a window, we could shift the window slightly in circles until the lock unlatched, letting us in. My dad would then have me crawl through the window to unlock the back door. He would dump out one or two of their trash cans into their back yard. We would then pile everything we wanted to steal into the empty trash cans. After loading up everything he wanted to take, we would put the trash cans up near the front yard before leaving. We would walk away from the house as if nothing had ever happened. Later that night, we would pull up in the truck with the lights off and the tailgate open. We would quickly walk up to the house, grab the trash cans full of loot, throw the entire cans into the truck, and drive away.

The more I did these things, the more he seemed to accept me as a person. He didn't hit me as often and didn't make fun of me as much. I almost felt like he was treating me like a son.

We started going out in the middle of the night as a family to construction sites. There we could steal copper wiring to recycle for money. He would take all of us to big open fields that were being structured for RV parks and housing developments. We would tie a chain from the back of his truck to a copper line buried in the ground. Then he would pull it up out of the ground by driving the truck slowly away. We would unearth truckloads of wiring from in the ground; load it into the bed of the truck and then drive out to abandoned canyons. Once in the canyons, we would mound all the copper wiring onto a pile of firewood. Then we would light the pile on fire and drive home. Because it was the middle of the night, no one would ever see the smoke from the fires. Before leaving the canyon to go home, my dad would drag a dead tree branch back and forth in the dirt where the canyon connected to the actual street. He would do this so in the morning we could see if anyone had driven into the canyon. As we would drive by the next day, he would peer out to see if there were any "fresh" tire prints going into the canyon. If there were any new tire prints, then he knew it was not safe to go back into the canyon. If there were no new prints, then we would rush back to collect all the newly burned wire.

After the plastic coating was all burned off, we would take it to the recycling centers for money. There were two reasons we burned the copper. The first reason was so that no one could ever trace where we had stolen the wire from. The second reason was because the recycling places gave a lot more money for the wire when the plastic coating was removed. The more money we made, the more drugs Warner could buy, which meant the happier he was and any abuse we would have to endure would lessen.

Unfortunately, I began to enjoy these opportunities to commit crimes with my dad. Although I had begun criminal actions with him in kindergarten, I was always somewhat hesitant to enjoy them. But now, I had begun to lose my innate innocence and started actually enjoying the thrill and excitement of breaking the law with him. The truth is, I became a really good thief, which helped our crimes become a fun challenge. He had always treated me horribly, but when I was working with or for him, I somehow felt more accepted by him, for a time. Anytime my dad needed help with his crimes and violence, I would jump at the opportunity to go with him. Since I had spent so many years helping my dad with his crimes, I became well versed in how to do these things. Whether it was arson, physical violence, robbery, or vandalism, I knew how to systematically think the crimes through, and how to lie if I was ever caught.

Without ever noticing, I was not only becoming more like him in my criminal actions, but I had also started thinking like him. I found myself actively looking for opportunities to continue his trainings, even when he was not instigating the actions. I began morphing into him, becoming more like him every day.

Just Taste It

Despite what actions I did to help or impress him, things never really changed at home. We were still treated as his property, his possessions, his slaves to torture when he felt it fit to do so. There was no escape for any of us, no matter what we did. My dad had beaten terror so deeply into us all that I feared even looking into his eyes. I never retaliated, I never "snitched" on him to the police, and I never told anyone anything about him. I knew there was nothing I could do to escape, so I never did anything that would upset him or make things any worse for my mom, sisters, and myself.

Even when we occasionally tried to escape to abuse shelters, we never actually told anyone there about any of the things he was doing to us. Our house only had a working telephone once in a while. We usually couldn't afford electricity, let alone a phone line. Despite this, anytime he suspected that I might talk to someone or "snitch" on him, he would drag me into the living room where he would slap me in the face with the handset part of the phone a few times before throwing the phone at me.

"Call CPS, you p*ssy. Call the police. Here, I'll even dial the number for you. Grow some balls, you little f*ggot. Call them!"

"I don't want to call anyone. I don't want them to know what I've done. I don't want to go to jail."

I would reassure him that I had no desire to ever "snitch" because then I would go to jail. When I placed the blame on myself and not him, he would feel better. It helped calm him down a little when I made it sound like it was me who was the problem and not him. I knew that even if I did snitch, both he and my mom would likely go to jail. At the same time, I assumed I would probably be sent to a Juvenile Hall and then my sisters would be sent to foster homes.

My dad had convinced me that life in a foster home would be far worse than living under his roof. My whole life, he told me what they do to foster kids and how bad their lives were. I would hear stories from him about how foster kids have to fight for their food, sleep on floors, don't have real homes, and don't have real families. I don't know why that frightened me so much, seeing that this was basically my life already. But I believed that if I were to ever call CPS, things would somehow be worse for me and my sisters. CPS would come to our house on occasion, but he had trained me to lie to them. My dad had taught me from an early age if I ever told them anything about him, they would only give him a warning and then leave. Once they were gone, he would "take care of me and my snitching." He made me believe that there was no possibility of escaping him. After all, "who would ever want to put up with a redheaded stepchild?" As an added safety, I would meet the CPS workers in the front yard so that they couldn't see inside the house. I would tell them my made-up stories of great dinners and a happy lifestyle at home.

Warner started becoming more and more aggressive as I got older. After I had turned thirteen years old, I truly believed that he had come to a point of actually trying to kill us. There was no more holding back for him in the things he would do to us.

There was a day that I was doing some work in the front yard for him. He came out and told me to try a bite of some guacamole he had made. He never cooked. I knew deep down that he had done something to the guacamole or had even poisoned it. I knew that if I ate any of it, I would probably die. I looked in his hand at the bowl to see if I could see the rat poison or anything else. It looked fine, but I still did not trust him. I knew he could have easily ground it up to hide it. He scooped a bite out with his pocketknife and stuck it in my face. I politely declined his offer and told him I didn't like guacamole. He became angry thrusting the knife forward at my face.

"Eat the f*cking bite!"

I started to back away shaking my head "No." In an instant, he thrust the knife at me, stabbing me in the stomach. Terrified at what just happened, I grabbed my stomach and looked down in horror. He didn't even look at me or the cut. He instantly turned and walked away. Fortunately, I was far enough from his reach for the blade not to cut deep enough to cause a mortal wound. It was however deep enough to draw blood and scare the life out of me. Now in a state of panic, I ran to the back of the house in case any neighbors happened to have seen anything. I didn't want anyone to call CPS, but I also didn't know how bad the cut was yet.

After I was safely hidden in the backyard, I checked my stomach to examine my wound. As I looked down at the bloody gash, I started crying. My imagination ran rampant with fears of what would come of this cut. As I stood huddled over against the wall crying, the older of my two sisters walked over to check on me. She had been outside playing when this all happened and sensed something was wrong. Being that she was only four years old at the time, she couldn't understand what had just happened. She only knew something was wrong and that I was hurt. I didn't want to scare or upset her, so I told her I was fine and sent her away from me. I knew she was now watching and so I fought to regain composure. After I finally stopped myself from crying, I went inside to clean myself up. Later that night, my parents brought their friend over to look at the cut. They told me she was a nurse, but I knew better. She asked me what happened in a way that made it clear to me that she didn't really care. I told her that I tripped while walking with scissors. She never even looked at the cut; she just asked me what happened and then smiled.

"Good boy, you look like you will be fine."

We began finding more and more poisonous items all throughout the house. Up until this point, my dad had only been targeting me or my mom, but now he seemed not to care who he hurt. The worst part was that he didn't try to hide his intentions, nor did he show any remorse for trying to hurt us.

My sisters were too young (three and four years old) to know what he was doing, requiring my mom and me to watch out for them and their safety around him. One evening, my older sister, not understanding that he enjoyed hurting us, asked our dad for some soda. She saw a soda bottle in the kitchen and so asked if she could have some.

"Dad, can I have some soda?"

"We don't have any soda."

"Yeah we do. There is a bottle on the kitchen table."

(Laughing) "Oh yeah, THAT soda. Yes, go ahead. You can have it all."

Excited, my sister ran into the house and took a big gulp from the bottle. She immediately started screaming and coughing in pain. Our dad stood several feet behind her laughing hysterically. He thought this was absolutely hilarious. My mom and I rushed in to help her. My mom told me to call 911, but our dad stopped me.

"It's fine. She just drank a little battery acid. It's nothing to be worried about. She will be fine."

My mom quickly mixed baking soda and water into a cup for my sister to drink, to help stop the burning.

Another time, my two sisters found and drank from a bottle of orange soda. My mom was freaking out and crying as both my sisters shook in horror. They crawled around in circles shaking and crying with pain. This time it wasn't battery acid. My dad had mixed some of his drugs (speed) into the orange soda and left it out. I don't know if he was hoping one of us would overdose and die, or if he hoped one of us would end up in the hospital. I know my mom used to mix her speed in with sodas. Perhaps he was trying to trap her for child endangerment. Most of his intentions were a mystery to us.

Either way, my mom was furious about this and began threatening to report him to the police. This caused him to become outraged and so he started locking us in our rooms to prevent us from being able to report him. He created locking mechanisms that he screwed into the walls above the doors so that we couldn't get out of the house. He also began secretly recording our every move when he was not home. At the time, we had no idea how he knew everything that was happening, but for the longest time, he was able to quote our exact words.

It wasn't until years later that we discovered some of the recording devices hidden inside the little beige plastic circular fire alarms. I don't know how or where he got them from, but he had somehow hidden them in every room of the house. Before we were aware of them, he would use the things he learned from the recordings to torment and strike fear into us.

If he was not home and I told my mother a story about something that happened at school, he would later say something that had to do with that conversation. If I asked permission to go to an event at the school like a football game, he would later come home and mention how fat I was and how I could not be seen in public because I would only embarrass us all.

"My god, look at your disgusting fat ass. I mean, you are so gross that you can't even do normal teenage things like go to a football game. Could you imagine yourself up in the bleachers? The school would lose money and get complaints because no one would be able to sit next to you. They would have to find a spot down in the dirt for you away from everyone. They couldn't even put you with the f*ggots and n*ggers because even they would not want to be near a redheaded stepchild."

He had discovered he could destroy us using our own words. All the secret things we said when he was not home were used against us. He would use these threats knowing we would think about them for weeks after. His threats and hurtful worlds would play over and over in my head. I started believing everything he said about me. Hiding my opinions, thoughts, and feelings from everyone, I found myself retracting from the world, trying to hide away from him and my worthless existence. I avoided going anywhere where there might be people. I never tried out for a sport, never went to a single sporting event with my school, never went to a single dance, play, concert, party etcetera. Warner's words made so insecure that I feared participating in any of the normal student activities.

Back to the Canyons

Throughout my earlier years of elementary school, my dad would put me in the corner of a room or in a closet and tell me not to move, then leave me there for a day or two. He would make me live in my own filth and starve for days at a time. I remember sitting on the floor (around first grade) bouncing on my bottom as I cried because I had to poop so badly. I didn't want to poop my pants because I feared how he would react, but I wasn't allowed to leave my spot to use the restroom. No matter how much I cried "I have to poop, I have to poop" he did not listen, and nobody cared.

As I grew into my later years of elementary school, he started taking me out to the canyons where he would do the same there. He would draw a circle in the sand around me and tell me not to move. Sometimes, he would just kick me out of the house and make me live on the front steps for a few days. This changed once my sisters were born. Because he *seemed* to care about his daughters, he started locking us in rooms inside the house and no longer outside or in the canyons. I usually occupied my time during these days by drawing, doing origami, or some other form of art.

It was during my eighth-grade year that he started hinting towards actually killing us again. He began cutting extension cords open so the wires would show, leaving guns out on the tables, or trying to get me to play with dangerous toys. He gave me a bow and arrow and then told me he would give me money if I could ever catch an arrow before it hit the ground after shooting it into the sky. He also taught me how I could throw a bullet into the ground to make it fire. He showed me this by holding a bullet with a pair of pliers off the edge of the concrete and then using a carpentry "punch" tool to strike the primer.

During one of the days when I was playing and practicing with his "teachings," I had a bullet fire after throwing it into a brick wall. The bullet struck me on the right side on my waist. When it hit me, I thought I had been stabbed with a hot ice pick. Luckily, the bullet only hit me and did not go through me. Even though it hurt horribly, I was able to clean myself up, hide my bruise, and carry on with life.

Another time, he started acting the same way he had on Thanksgiving Day in 6th grade when my grandpa shot him. He took all of us down to a canyon where we would burn our copper. He made my mom stay in the truck while he pulled my sisters and me out. He drew a circle in the sand around us and told us not to move, then jumped back into the truck and drove off with my mom. I could see my mom was worried and against him leaving us, but she knew better than to question or fight him. As they drove off, I told my sisters to stay close to me. I knew that if we moved, he would see our footprints and know that we strayed. This was one of the hardest times I had with my sisters. We were ages fourteen, four, and three years old. We only had one bottle of water and nothing else. We stayed in the circle all through the first night. It was freezing cold in the middle of the night and the dirt hurt to sleep on. I barely slept that night because I was so afraid of coyotes, scorpions, or any other creatures getting us in the night. I did the best I could to keep my sisters safe and warm.

The next morning, we had to move to get out of the sun. As we wandered around the canyon, I found a pile of ashes from a previous fire. I didn't recognize this pile as one of our copper burning piles, so out of boredom, I began poking at the charred remnants with a stick. While doing so, I flipped over a burned board from in the fire. Underneath was a half-burned baby picture of me. I realized in that moment that we were in real danger. I knew he was going to kill us that day. He was erasing our existence by burning everything. I grabbed my sisters and began to run with them towards the main streets, out of the canyon.

We almost made it out of the canyon before Warner pulled up in the truck and grabbed us. I immediately told him that his daughters needed water to help distract him from finding out that we had found the pictures. I explained that we only left the circle because his daughters needed help. He never said a word to us. The whole drive was in absolute silence. I was in a panic of terror because I couldn't tell what his game plan was.

He took us back up to our house in Morongo Valley where he had locked my mom up. When we got there, he ordered us to stay in the truck while he got our mom. He jumped out and ran into the house. A moment later, he burst out the front door, dragging our mom behind him by her hair. She screamed and fought to get away, but he was too powerful. He dragged her over to the truck where he jumped into the driver's seat, ordering her to get in.

As she opened her door to get into the passenger seat, he reached over and grabbed her by the hair and started driving. She was not yet all the way in the truck before he started driving. He pinned her head tightly to the passenger seat so that she could not get in or break free. He continued to drive while dragging her outside of the truck. My sisters were screaming in horror as they attempted to stop him by hitting and screaming. I fought to keep my sisters away from their dad as he drove us recklessly down the highway, all while dragging their mother outside of the truck by her hair. She was kicking and screaming in pain, while passing cars honked and screamed at us.

He drove us out to a canyon where he threw me out of the truck before continuing on with my mom and sisters. He took them far into the canyon before he stopped and then dragged them out into the sand. He started hitting my mother telling her that they were all going to die that day. He pinned her down and then grabbed my little sisters to force them next to her. My sisters were screaming and fighting back but could not stop him. He pulled out a hammer and forced it into my sisters' hands. Bouncing back and forth between both girls, he wrapped their little fingers around the handle and then held his hand round theirs so that they could not let go. He then made both of my sisters take turns hitting their mother in the head. No matter how loud they screamed or fought against him, they could not stop him or run away. He was screaming out at them that they were going to "help mommy go to sleep." He made my sisters take turns trying to kill their own mother with a hammer.

After several minutes of this, he finally told her he was done and was ready to kill her. He stood up and grabbed a big rock to crush my mom's head. When he hoisted the rock up over his head, the desert heat in combination with his physical explosion must have caused him heat exhaustion and dehydration because he passed out and fell backwards onto the desert floor. My mother grabbed my sisters and started crawling out to the highway. By this time, I had gotten help from passing cars on the highway. Someone called 911 for us ensuring that the police were coming. They arrested Warner and took the rest of us to the hospital.

Although my sisters were very young, only one was able to forget this day. The older of my two sisters remembers every detail of being forced to take turns with the hammer trying to kill her own mother. I would love to say that he went to prison that day, we were saved, and that everything got better after that. But it didn't.

My mom was too afraid of him to press charges, ensuring him his freedom a few days later. We spent a few weeks in an abuse shelter and then ended up right back at home with him, tied tightly into the same routine.

Something Snapped

By eighth grade, I was angry, hurt, and lost. The more bitterness I lived through, the deader I became inside. I started hanging out with other kids who shared the same hatred for life. These were the kids who would openly cause problems. As long as I was with these kids, the "pot heads" and "skaters" I was somewhat comfortable. They didn't expect good grades or real friendships. Within these groups, there was no need for self-worth, as we would look for ways to express our rebellion and hatred.

Most of my time with these kids was spent doing drugs. Sometimes we would break into houses we knew were empty and then drink bottles of vodka mixed with cool aid that I had stolen for us. Other times, we would smoke pot and then run around town ripping Christmas lights down off of houses. We would walk up to the house, grab the cable of lights, and then pull it while running as fast as we could so that all of the lights would crash into the ground. Or we'd drop acid at the bus stop before school, then make other kids fight. We would grab each other's hands and form a circle around two kids and then force them fight each other. Sometimes we would offer to get someone high and then make them smoke horse manure. Other times we would break random windshields or throw rocks into the highway at passing cars before running off to hide.

Whenever any of us would get upset with someone else in the group, we would fight. It was a "dog-eat-dog" group of kids where every person had to watch out for themselves. Within these groups, there was no need for self-worth, as we would verbally abuse each other as well as others. We were all horrid to each other.

But when I was with these groups of people, I felt comfortable. I knew how to act with them, and they all treated me exactly how I felt inside. As long as I acted like my dad, they seemed to accept me. In these groups, outsiders would generalize us all as one group rather than individually troubled kids, some of whom had been abused. This helped to take the individual emphasis off of my problems and blame us all as a group. Without an awareness of what was occurring and against my personal desires, I was becoming just like my dad.

Eventually, people outside of my "friend group" started to treat me differently. They started avoiding me more than before. People started whispering about me as if I were my dad. They began to fear me and the things that I might do. I didn't like this because I hated my dad more than anything in this world. He would tear me down emotionally and then hit me for fun. I would lie in bed at night with a deep, burning hatred clouding my thoughts. I would lie there, imagining ways he could die or ways that I could kill him. I would lie in bed, flexing the muscles in my hands and arms as hard as I could without making a sound, as I lied there crying and wishing for my own death. I knew this wasn't an option though because I couldn't bear the idea of leaving my sisters with him.

I would imagine walking into my dad's room with a baseball bat while he slept. I envisioned myself quietly creaking open his bedroom door, then sneaking over to his bed while he lay there asleep. I would stare down at him as he slept.

I could see myself raising the bat over my head before I began beating his skull with the bat. In my imagination, I could feel and smell his blood splattering all over me as I beat him to death. I could feel the warmth of his blood covering my hands, arms, and face. I could taste his blood as it splattered into my mouth. I would lay there flexing my hands into fists as I imagined gripping the bat. I would imagine gripping the bat so tightly, that it would cause my fingernails to dig into the palms of my hands. I would clench my jaw so tight that my teeth would hurt. I would wake up in the mornings with extreme headaches and cuts on my palms from straining my fists and clenching my jaw during the night. I would imagine this scenario over and over every night as I tried to go to sleep. I was often exhausted the next morning and at school because of this.

When I started to realize that people thought I was becoming just like him, I freaked out.

I suddenly had a horrible feeling deep inside as if he were part of me. I could feel him inside my chest, in my gut, and all over in my skin. I started developing obsessive compulsive behaviors of trying to wash him out of me. No matter how hard I tried, I couldn't seem to wash him out of me. I would scrub and scratch at my hands, arms, and legs, trying to scrape him out.

Because we seldom had running water in the house, bathing and laundry were nearly impossible. To combat this, I started stealing water from neighbor's houses in the middle of the night. I would sneak over late at night to fill five-gallon buckets with water from their hose spigots in order to clean myself. I would bring the buckets of water into my backyard where I would boil the water in a pot over a fire pit and then wash myself with a rag. After I was clean, I would wash my clothes for the next day. Because I only had a few articles of clothing, I would have to do this several times a week. After washing my clothes, I would hang them out to dry for the rest of the night on a chain-link fence. The next day, I would shiver all through the morning as my cold, wet clothes continued to dry on my body. Whenever we had electricity, I would dry my clothes with an old paint removal gun. It would stink so badly of burning metal and would get scorching hot, but it worked to dry my clothes.

I also started scrubbing my room clean on a daily basis. I would scrub my carpet with a hand brush and Simple Green. Afterwards, I would clean my walls and then every belonging I had in my room. *I was trying to wash him out of me. No matter how hard I scrubbed, I could still feel him inside of me and so I would start over and scrub everything again.*

Even though cleaning became an obsession for me, I never felt clean. My original blue carpet had eventually become a silver shade of white from being scrubbed so much. I also started to get the feeling that I had no control in my life. To help with my own insecurities in this, I started overly organizing things. I would organize my few possessions by categories, alphabetical order, sizes, shapes, in whatever systems I could concoct. Then I would scrub them clean and re-organize them. Warner still had me go with him to do his callings, but in secret, I would try to wash him out.

By this point of my life, I was fourteen years old, and Warner had trained me to be a highly proficient thief. On a nearly daily basis, he would coach me through stealing thousands of dollars' worth of merchandise at a time. My original shopping lists of random items had become bottles of vodka, full racks of ribs, and small electronic devices. Eventually, this grew until he had taught me how to steal large quantities of things from large shopping centers. I would have to steal pallets worth of electronic devices at a time from places like K-Mart. These stores would roll full pallets onto the store floor from in the back just before closing so that they could re-stock the shelves. I was a pretty good thief by third grade but now, I was a highly proficient professional.

As we became more confident with our shopping center *runs* we became more aggressive in our tactics. We followed the different security cars to learn what stores they checked in on every night and what times they would drive by. I would go into the garden section of these stores towards closing time.

These stores all did the same thing before closing hours. They would put a chain and lock on the back doors going out into the outside gated garden area. I would bring my own lock (same brand and look as theirs) and then "dummy lock" the doors with my lock. "Dummy locking" is when you push the lock almost shut so that it looks locked, but it's not. The employees would see that the doors were already "locked" and then leave them alone. I would then hide somewhere in the store and wait for them to close. These stores only had security cameras watching the cash registers and the main exit doors.

This meant that the back doors to the garden were always an easy route for me.

Once the store closed to the public, I could sneak out of my hiding place to open the back door. I would then roll pallets of merchandise out to the garden area. During the night, they would do re-stocking which made it easy to move full pallets outside. As long as I was careful not to be seen, no one ever knew I was there. Once everything was outside in the garden area, I would put everything up on top of the pallets of manure, then climb over the fence, bringing everything with me.

My dad would pull up to the back-parking lot for me to load everything into the truck. In a matter of seconds, we would be gone with our new merchandise. We were smart in the fact that we never took too much. It was usually one pallet filled with individual $100 cordless razors, or VCR's, or something like that. It was always just enough for him to sell for more drug money, but not enough to be traced back to us.

Most nights went like clockwork as we ran our routine. My whole family would enter the store near to closing time. We would walk around the store acting like we were shopping. My mom would purchase a few small items before she left the store. If we didn't need anything, she would purchase some random item that she could return for her money back the next day.

While we were doing the shopping, my dad would keep an eye out for a full pallet. If there wasn't a full pallet on the floor, he would load up a cart or two and then abandon them in an aisle towards the back-garden area before he left. We always made sure that my dad entered and exited the store apart from us so that no one would ever know we were together. This was an added protection for him in case I ever got caught. Then I would dummy lock the back before I hid away. My mom and sisters would check out and then leave the store without me.

As much as I hated my dad and hated having to do as he commanded, there was a feeling of adventure, intensity, and excitement every time I would have to steal the big amounts.

It was like being on a rollercoaster without a seatbelt; not knowing if you would make it out alive. I felt like I was in a spy movie as I snuck my way back to the garden without being seen before carefully removing the chain and lock from the back doors without making a sound. I'd quietly sneak a pallet jack from the back of the garden area into the store to grab a loaded pallet. On the nights that there was no pallet, I would sneak the pre-filled heaping shopping carts outside. I would sit in silence for what felt like hours sometimes, waiting for a clear moment to do my job.

My absolute favorite part was outside of the store in the garden area. Once alone, my heart would race as I loaded the items up onto the shelves of planting manure. Once everything was loaded, I awaited the big escape. Before I would leave though, I'd push the carts or empty pallet jack neatly up into a corner so that no one would find them in the morning and grow suspicious.

One night, while we were on one of these special *shopping trips*, I had my older sister who was barely five years old in my cart. My mom had my other sister in her cart as we walked around. My sister and I left my mom and other sister so that we could look around in the toys before it was time to get to work. A store employee started following my mom as if they knew something sketchy was happening with her. To protect herself, she took my youngest sister out of the cart and left the store without purchasing anything. When she left, I was unsure of what to do and so my sister and I quickly snuck out into the garden area. I figured that they were probably still watching my mom, so I quickly rolled our loaded shopping carts out into the back to steal.

My sister sat in silence as I quickly loaded everything up to take. Once everything was up on the shelves, I realized that I didn't know how to get my sister out with me. There was a large green electrical transformer just outside the metal bars of the garden fence. I hopped up over the fence and moved a few items onto the transformer so that there was a clearing large enough to get my sister out with me. Afterwards, I grabbed my sister and carefully helped her climb over with me.

Once over the fence, I started collecting all of our items and stacking them for a quick pick up with the truck after. There were still several large boxes sitting on the transformer. I had four or five tall stacks of boxed electronics and other items stacked up on the ground next to it. Suddenly, a police car pulled up in the back alleyway and stopped next to us. My heart sank. There was no way I could run away fast enough and still hold onto my sister. Normally, I would hop back over the fence and then escape through the front of the store. As long as I didn't have anything on my person when I left the store, I technically had not stolen anything, therefor wouldn't be arrested. But this was not a possibility while I had my sister with me.

Not knowing what to do, I hid my sister behind the transformer with me and began to prepare her for the cops to come get us. I tried explaining to her that they were going to drive us to the station for mom and dad to come pick us up. I didn't want her to be afraid, so I was preparing her for what was about to happen. I assured her that nothing was wrong and that the police were only there to help us get home safely.

We sat there in silence, barely making a sound as we breathed. But to my surprise, they never came out to get us. They pulled their car up next to us, then turned the engine off and sat there. I couldn't figure out what was going on. The two policemen were sitting inside of their car only ten feet away from us. I had stacks of stolen items sitting in plain sight only five feet from them. Still, they never came. My sister and I sat for what felt like an eternity, quietly fretting our impending doom.

After nearly an hour, the police car suddenly started and then they drove away. I grabbed my sister and started running as fast as I could while carrying her. We ran to our normal pickup spot a few blocks away where my parents had been sitting, watching, waiting. As we jumped into the truck, I could barely talk from how out of breath I was. Both of my parents burst out laughing. I could see my dad wanted to say something, despite his laughter.

"Did you sh*t your pants?"

"Yeah, I think so," I said chuckling nervously.

"Us too," he said while laughing and celebrating.

"What happened, why were they there like that?"

"They must have been on a break or doing paperwork or something."

"What about you Mom, did they bust you?"

"No, they were just suspicious. Nothing to worry about."

My dad drove my mom and sisters home before he and I drove back to pick up the stacks of stuff.

But not every night out was a success. There were nights I would have to run from employees after being seen and then we would have to avoid that store for months after. Some days, I was unable to fulfill my quota of stolen merchandise, giving Warner a reason to punish me. This often consisted of him threatening to turn me into the police for all the shoplifting I had just done, before being locked in my room for a length of time. Sometimes this was a day or two, while other times it would be for weeks. His final warning on these days would be spoken in a calm and steady voice and not yelled, which was somehow even scarier.

"Get out of my sight your worthless piece of sh*t, and don't let me see you again."

Whenever I heard this, I knew not to come out until he called for me, no matter how long that may be. However, I knew that if I missed school, then we chanced having CPS come to the house. This would never end well for any of us and so I would sneak out in the mornings to still go to school. I was now in ninth grade, ensuring that the school would report students for truancies.

Whenever I was helping to steal truckloads for Warner, I would always add my own personal items to the list. As long as it was only one or two things here and there, my dad did not mind. I began secretly collecting art supplies and books. When I did get in trouble and restricted to my room, I would utilize the art supplies to occupy myself. I became very good at different forms of art due to the abundance of time I had to practice. I also began stealing music CDs and boxes of candy bars so that I could turn around and resell them at school. The money I made from these sales was used to purchase popular name brand clothing in an attempt to stay clean and fit in at school. I hated the fact that I had to be like him by stealing to break free, but I knew it was the best option I had if I truly wanted to avoid becoming just like him.

Get A Job

In my freshman year of high school, my dad started working at a local Mobil gas station. I never really understood what made him decide to get a job, as he never held a standard job as far as I could remember. I could assume that he took it as an opportunity to rob the store of alcohol (which he did), but we could have easily done that without him having to work there. Was it possible that he used this as a drug front or a way to launder larger amounts of drugs and money? I can't say for sure, but I knew he had his reasons. He would never miss an opportunity to con his way for his own benefit. Afterall, this was the man that I watched nearly drown himself to win money in a lawsuit.

Several years earlier, we were visiting my dad's parents' house. They lived in a mobile home park that had an indoor community pool. I loved visiting them because we would nearly always get to go swimming. On this day, my dad saw that there was some light construction being done to a window in the room. After excusing himself to use the restroom, he quickly grabbed a small handful of screws and placed them next to the pool's edge. When returning from the restroom, he stepped on the screws, screamed out in pain, and fell into the pool, landing on the edge of the pool with his rib cage. Once in the water, he began to breathe deep in an attempt to drown himself. One of the other adults in the pool raced over to rescue him from drowning. The man "saved his life" before calling 911. An ambulance came and took my dad to the hospital for his foot, ribs, and near drowning. Warner filed an incident report and then sued the mobile home park. I remember him laughing at the whole scenario and saying the only bad part was the IV they put in his hand. His years of shooting up had destroyed his veins causing the paramedic to have to try multiple painful attempts before finding success.

As stated before, Warner never seemed to have any reason for working a real job. He made his money by selling stolen goods and performing conniving little stunts like the pool incident, which he successfully won. He had an ulterior motive for working at the Mobile station, but it was never made known to any of us.

A few weeks into my dad's new job, the owner discovered that my dad was in fact stealing large quantities of alcohol. Of course, he fired him. This, most likely, would not have been a big deal except for the owner who decided to call my dad a few racial slurs in the heat of the moment while firing him. The owner could clearly see my dad was extremely racist by his tattoos, but in his moment of anger, he called Warner a string of racial slurs. These slurs set my dad off into a fit of rage.

My dad never said a word to any of us about getting fired. We all carried on with life as if nothing had changed. But not Warner. He had plans for revenge. That night, my dad snuck back down to the gas station. He placed homemade explosives around the outside of the minimart portion of the gas station and then lit the structure on fire. He knew that the fire would catch and then spread to the gas bombs he placed around the property. As our little town of fourteen hundred people peacefully slept, he quickly drove away from the burning flames. Suddenly a loud explosion broke the midnight silence.

The gas station roared with out-of-control flames as gas bombs exploded into the night. Normally, my dad was extremely smart and a talented criminal. This time however was different. He was angry as he retaliated in haste without a pre-planned strategy as he normally did. He made multiple mistakes which made it easy for the police to track the person responsible.

The next morning, there was a huge crash at my front door. The house shook as the loud noise abruptly woke us all from our rest. It was the sound of a team of policemen kicking in the front door before racing into my parent's bedroom. They tackled my dad as he tried jumping to his feet to flee. My mom, sisters and I all stood dumbstruck as we watched them arrest him, and then drag him out into the police car. I had seen him arrested many times before, but never had I seen the cops kick in our front door. My mom and I looked at each other with the slight hint of a smile as they drove him away. I didn't know what he had done, but something told me that this was the last time I would ever have to see him.

For the first time in my life, I actually believed that we were all going to be freed from Warner and his tyranny. I believed that my mom would actually have a chance at life and wouldn't go back to him after. The courts held Warner with a one-hundred-thousand-dollar bail, which we did not have, and so he had to remain detained until the actual hearing. It was several months later at the hearing when the judge sentenced my dad to many years in prison for arson that my mom began to feel the same way. She immediately stopped doing drugs, stopped smoking, started going to church, and sought out help to gain her freedom.

The first few weeks were the hardest as my mom fought against her addictions and we all fought to figure out what our new life was. We had the chance at a new life; a chance to find acceptance within society, and not to live in daily fear. We were not sure what that meant for us exactly, but we were excited to find out.

One of the first things I did after Warner was taken away, was to change my name back to Jason Powell. After a lifetime of being "Jake Dawson" I was finally able to break free of the identity he constructed for me. I finally had a chance to erase Jake Dawson from the planet, and erase the person Warner had created, molded, and terrorized into resembling himself.

I collected all artifacts I could find with the name Jake on them and burned them. As I stood over the fire watching all physical remnants of Jake Dawson burn into nothingness, I began a new start as Jason Powell. This became a permanent feeling of accomplishment a year later when I earned a driver's license with *my real name* on it.

With Warner now being gone and my identity switching over to Jason Powell, I would love to say that I was suddenly different, but I wasn't. I truly wanted to be different, but after years of being trained to become a man just like my dad, I could not seem to break free of him. I still treated others horribly, and still found refuge within problem groups. I stopped the drugs, alcohol, and illegal activities, but still hung out with those people. No matter what the outward changes I was striving to make, I was still angry. The only major change for me now was that I didn't have to fear Warner every time I came home.

Redemption?

Before my dad was sent to prison, there was a young man up the street who used to drive by everyday waving to us. I never understood why he was so nice to us, knowing we were such awful people. Most people feared my family and avoided making any kind of contact with us, but not this guy. In fact, he was the same young man who had given us the dishes of food right after Thanksgiving when my dad was shot.

Whenever he would drive by and wave, my dad would make fun of him.

"Hey look, there goes the little queer again. I should kill that little f*ggot for trying to flirt with us."

I was always hesitant to wave back and often wondered why he was so insistent on being kind to us. Perhaps he simply did not know who we were or what we were known as? At the very least, I knew he was aware of some of my dad's past, due to the huge "child molester" billboard in my neighbor's yard. I figured he must not have been aware of all the other things we were known for. Everyone in town knew who Warner was and thought my family was dangerous, but maybe no one else had warned him? For whatever reason, this young man did not seem to care and would wave to us every day as he passed by.

Shortly after Warner was arrested for the Mobile Station arson, this young man stopped by my school bus stop one morning. He handed all of us at the bus stop a flyer to come to his church youth group. The flyer said, "Come meet Jesus" and "Jesus loves you." We all laughed at him and threw the papers away, making fun of him and his "God." Inside, I was furious. I was beyond upset at this man for saying that "Jesus loved us." How could he have the audacity to claim that God, or anyone else for that matter, cared about me? He had no idea the things that I had done, or the things that had been done to me. Who did he think he was, trying to claim that Jesus loved me? I was the unwanted, redheaded stepchild, burden on my family.

Dr. Jason Powell

I ignored the young man week after week as he handed out flyers and invited me to his church. Eventually, I started feeling guilty for being so angry with him. After all, this was the guy who not only fed my entire family at Thanksgiving after Warner was shot but he was also the only person to ever really be nice to my family. He was the guy who always waved to us as he drove by. Eventually I gave in and attended his youth group.

At first, I hated it there. In the beginning, the other kids were rude to me and avoided me, making sure that I knew I didn't belong there. I attended every week though because the young man who invited me was kind and would always feed us cookies and soda during his Bible teachings. Eventually, I started making friends in the group as kids started seeing and treating me differently.

He would ask us random questions at the start of each meeting as a way of "breaking the ice" before the lesson began. Some of the questions were really hard for me.

"Ok guys, the question tonight is: Who has the best French fries?"

Different kids argued In-N-Out, Jack in the Box, Del Taco etc. I had no idea what any of these places' French fries tasted like and so I kept silent.

At first, I tried to have him skip me when it was my turn to answer his question. He never allowed me to "pass" on my turn no matter how much I tried. After I would reluctantly answer, he would always comment on how great my answer was and how much he appreciated it. Again, I could not figure out why he was so nice to me, but I secretly loved it. It was one of the first times in my sixteen years of life that I was invited to leave my childhood life from which my voice had been stolen. And it was one of the first times I learned I had a voice worthy of being heard. All my life, I was coerced into oppression by my dad and made to believe I was stupid and worthless. I never had a voice or any value, but it was different when I was at youth group. There, I was acknowledged, appreciated, encouraged, and treated nicely.

Babies and Tumors

My mom had always been a large person in size, weighing over three hundred pounds for most of my life. It wasn't more than a month or so after Warner's arrest that my mom started to feel something was wrong in her body. She feared that she possibly had developed a tumor or even cancer. Checking for her safety, she had me take her to the hospital.

The doctor notified her that she was nearly six months pregnant. My mom argued with the doctor, explaining that she had her ovarian tubes cut and tied to prevent pregnancy five years earlier. She had been smoking, drinking, and doing speed up until Warner's arrest, only a few weeks earlier. The doctor told her they were going to have to do an emergency c-section to save the baby. Warner's third daughter, my third little sister was born nearly two months premature; weighing just five pounds, nine ounces. My little sister spent several weeks in the hospital before she was strong enough to live outside of constant medical help.

Once my mom and new baby sister were released to come home, it was my job to take care of them. The nurses taught me how to change the gauze in my mom's c-section cut. She would have to help me lift the large flap of fat from her stomach so that I could get to the incision. It was always jarring to me how badly it smelled while doing this. I would put on gloves and then reach up under her belly flap into the incision. I would pull out yards and yards of bloody gauze before I could clean her. I would then wipe away as much of the brownish, yellowish iodine as I could from her wound before dumping hydrogen peroxide onto it. After a moment of letting it bubble, I would wipe all of the excess hydrogen peroxide. Once it was all cleaned up, I would have to put new iodine on her, then shove new gauze into the cut. Because my mom was in so much pain and too large to walk, I also had to help her with her bodily waste. I had to force a bed pan down under her when she needed to relieve herself and then wipe her clean after.

I would bring her a pot of warm water and a washcloth to bathe, but she could only reach some parts of her body, leaving me to do the rest for her. By this time, my two older sisters were five and six years old. Because of their age, my mom and I often asked for their help with these things. Neither of them hesitated to take on some of the burdens of things like helping to clean our mom up and help her go to the bathroom. Luckily, she had made enough friends in the church by now to have people stopping by to help. We had several people prepare meals to give us, while others would stop by to help with whatever I couldn't do while at school. However, the bulk of the burden fell on my sisters and me.

The one nice thing about having to take care of my mother during this time was that we became really close. We had always been as close as Warner would allow, but now we were becoming friends. We would talk for hours about anything and everything we could. I would tell her about my day, and she would share stories about the shows she was watching on television. My mom was becoming my best friend. After years of living in pain together under Warner's control, it was a gift to enjoy some freedom and happiness together.

Fat Fingers

I was out skateboarding with a friend toward the start of my sophomore year of high school, when my friend needed to use the bathroom. We quickly skateboarded over to his house. While he was in the bathroom, I noticed a guitar sitting in the corner of the living room. As I looked at it, I noticed that the tuners were all out of line from each other, so I "fixed" them for him by straightening them all into one clean line. As I was doing this, he came out of the bathroom and saw me.

"Dude, what are you doing, you messed it up. It's going to be completely out of tune now."

"No man, I just straightened them all up."

"No, you just detuned it."

As it turned out, I was in fact actually de-tuning the guitar. After explaining this to me, he taught me to play my first song on the guitar. He taught me to play *Smoke on the Water* from "Deep Purple."

My whole life had been filled with different little interactions with music, which had always excited me. I had always been interested in music and wanted to play but was never given the opportunity to truly dive in. During my time of living with my aunt in second grade, I learned to play a little piano. I also got to see my cousin playing flute which made me look forward to 6th grade when I too could play an instrument. Unfortunately, Warner did not allow me to play an instrument in 6th grade, but now he was gone. I finally had an opportunity to learn.

When my friend taught me this song on the guitar, I was absolutely enamored. I told him that I was going to go buy a guitar and start playing. He laughed at me and told me that I could not be a guitarist because I had "fat little hands with fat little fingers" and that "you have to have long skinny fingers to play the guitar." As he said this to me, all I heard was my dad coming from his mouth. My friend's comments were the same negative put-downs that I had finally been released from with my dad's recent arrest. But I would not let these words have the same effect on me that Warner's had. My friend's statement drove a determination deep into me. I went home and put everything I owned into a wagon and walked down to the local Pawn Shop.

When I got to there, I told the guy working in the pawn shop I would trade him everything I owned for a guitar. The clerk laughed at me, but then started looking at the things I had to offer and eventually made me a deal. He took the things I had to offer that were worth any money, and then had me pull some weeds around the property in trade for a cheap children's guitar. I was so excited that I became glued to my new guitar. Every moment of every day was filled with me exploring how to play. With absolute determination, I started working to prove my friend (and Warner) wrong by becoming a good guitarist. I set out to prove that I was *not*, in fact, worthless.

In a few short weeks my mother, teachers, and school acquaintances noticed my guitar playing and began acknowledging my new talent. My mom started encouraging me to come with her to church because "there were kids who played on the worship team" there. I decided to join her to see for myself. While there, one of the worship team kids invited me to join them at practice on Thursday nights. I of course, did not pass up this opportunity.

Music was not just a hobby to me; it instantly became an identity. I began playing in every opportunity I could find. As I started showing signs of talent on the guitar, the young man that led the church group started asking me to bring my guitar with me to youth group so that we could "jam" after. He played the drums and so after youth group, he would ask me to show him the songs I learned that week. The youth pastor was always so excited to see what I'd learned and would encourage me to play more. After I got the songs started on my guitar, he would join me on his drums. After a few months of playing, he invited me to play with him during worship for his youth group. With Warner now gone from my life, this new life was an actual possibility for me. I excitedly exclaimed, "Yes!"

My whole life up to this point felt like a punishment. I spent so many years feeling angry and believing that I had no purpose or belonging. I spent so many years wishing for death, yet now, things were changing. I had moved into a place of being trusted with a leadership position at youth group. The youth leader chose me, of all people, to help with leading his group. I began living every moment of my life looking forward to Wednesday nights and Sunday mornings when I would get to play my guitar with the other musicians. I had finally found acceptance by helping to lead worship in these groups. After a short while, this led to all of us worship team kids starting our own little garage band.

Every time I played, people complimented me, accepted me as a member of the group, looked beyond who my father was, and treated me like an actual person. I was no longer just a red headed stepchild. When I played music, people stopped regarding me in negative ways. This man, who used to just wave as he drove by my house, somehow gave me a purpose and desire in life.

A Mission

No longer under Warner's constant control, my mom and I became best friends as we explored our way through our new lives. She encouraged and supported me in my musical pursuits, and I supported and encouraged her as she began the divorce process. It amazed me how terrified we both were during the entire divorce. Warner was locked up in prison, yet we were both still having nightmares and were terrified of what he was going to do to us. We both knew deep down that if he ever got out of jail, we would all be dead. We knew that he would seek revenge on my mom for divorcing him and on us for supporting her. Even still, we had to be strong if we really wanted to break free.

We were trying our hardest, but we both had many years of anguish, pain, and anger built up in us, and so we struggled to figure out our new lives and new roles. We often had long drawn-out fights resulting in me leaving or her kicking me out.

We would say horrible things to each other and call each other names in attempts to hurt one another. We loved each other and had become best friends, but old habits die hard. After our fights, I would leave for a few hours, giving us both some time to collect ourselves. I would then come home and we would be good again.

My youth pastor invited me to go to a convention with the youth group in San Diego for an entire weekend. This was not only a chance to get away from my family for a weekend, but it was also a chance to hang out with my new friends from church. While at this youth convention, the organization shared a video of how we could all join them in an international mission trip. When I saw this video, I was instantly enthralled with the thought that I could actually be part of something so amazing. The video showed kids from America going all over the world to other countries to help other people.

Of course, every kid at the convention wanted to go on a trip. When I got home, I explained the whole idea to my mother. She was supportive of the idea and encouraged me to try to do it. We looked through the options and decided that if I could raise the money, I should go to Panama for the summer. We chose this country because it was the cheapest of the options available. The total trip cost was just over $2,000 for a full month mission trip in Panama. Honestly, neither my mom nor I thought I would be able to raise that kind of money, but figured it was at least worth a try.

The next three months of my life revolved around fundraising. My fundraising included car washes, yard work, bake sales, and other typical teenage fundraising ideas. The one thing that amazed me the most was when I began walking door-to-door asking for donations. The people in my town knew who I was and the family from which I came. I had been isolated for so long, I expected people to slam their doors in my face in fear or disgust, but what I found was a community of people who were friendly, loving, and forgiving. People were so supportive of my breaking free of my father and his way of life, that they were more than willing to help in achieving my goal. I not only raised enough money for Panama, but also enough to spend the following summer on another church trip in Botswana, Africa.

Many times, people would tell me that they saw me all the time out on the streets pulling my sisters around in a wagon or stroller. This was funny to me because I never saw any of these people ever taking notice of me. If anything, I always thought they were turning away to avoid me in disgust.

All those years, when my dad was home, I feared that he would beat or kill anyone who was in his way. My sisters were only babies at the time and so I would save them by walking them up and down the streets of our town for hours at a time. I did not care what the weather was like. It would be better to be out on the streets than at home where we might have been killed. Getting them out of the house was my way of saving all of our lives. I don't know how, but people seemed to know what I was doing and took great compassion on me. The people in the community fully rallied behind me and my breaking free of my past.

At the time, I would have argued that I was going on these trips to help others. I would have argued that these were selfless acts of kindness from me because of the new person I was becoming. In hindsight, I can see that this was actually my way of trying to leave my past behind. I was trying to get as far away from who I was before by not only doing good deeds, but also by going as far away as possible.

During my time in Panama and Africa, I saw impoverished families living in third-world-country environments. I saw children who shared similarities to what my sisters and I lived in back home. Ultimately, I saw that no matter how bad my life may have seemed to me, I was not alone. These trips opened my eyes to see that I had a choice of being a victim or a victor. Helping these families overseas helped me see that change was possible and that no one is helpless to make changes in their own lives.

As time went on, my mother continued to grow in size. Years of abuse, drugs, and alcohol took a toll on her mentally and physically. By my junior year of high school, she had grown to well over five hundred pounds and was having a hard time doing pretty much anything. I started having to take care of the family in every way. I did all the shopping, cooking, cleaning, and everything else that was needed in a family. My mom started experiencing pains all over her body so badly that she was unable to sleep at night. She would spend entire nights awake, crying out in pain. My sisters and I could all hear her suffering but had no way of easing her pain. All of us did everything we could to help her throughout each day. Because my two older sisters were around seven and eight years old, they had become really good at helping their mom as well. Our youngest sister was only two years old and so she was unable to help.

I could tell the pain was getting worse with every passing day because my mom would go through sudden mood swings.

One moment she would be screaming that she hated me and wished I was never born, then the next moment she would be apologizing for everything she made me live through. One of my worst memories at this point in our lives was when we watched the movie "What's Eating Gilbert Grape." My mom projected the whole movie onto me and blamed herself for ruining my life. The film told the story of an overweight mother who needed her oldest child to take care of her and the family. The mother in the film blamed herself for ruining their lives. In the end, the mother dies and so the family burns the house down around her to avoid making a spectacle of her size. My own mother started asking me to burn our house down around her. She would promise me that it would not hurt as she would suffocate before the flames got to her. She would continually apologize to me for "being a spectacle" and destroying my life, before begging me to help her die by burning the house down on her.

As she would pour out tears and apologies to me, I wanted nothing more than to burst into tears with her. I had watched her suffer with abusive beatings from Warner my entire life, but this felt worse. She was no longer just praying for death; she was now literally begging me to help her in it. Her pains were now the pains of a person who had given up on life. As much as it hurt me to see and hear her like this, I had to put my self-concerns aside. I had no choice but to put on a brave face and be strong for my mom and three little sisters.

Broken Gurneys &
Math Problems

It was the first day of my second semester in senior year of high school. I was running late for school when I was pulled over by an undercover policeman for speeding. Luckily for me, the officer let me go with only a warning and a small lecture.

After serving my first period detention for arriving to school late, I went about my day as usual. Hours later, just after my lunch break, I had my first day in a new math class. As I opened the door, I was shocked to see the policeman that had pulled me over earlier that morning sitting in the front of the room. The bell had not rung yet and so students were still walking in and socializing with each other. The officer called me up to the front of the room where he quietly started talking with me.

"Hello Mr. Dawson, why don't you come sit up here with me."

I thought for sure I was in some serious trouble. At first, I wondered if maybe he was there to give me a real ticket after all. Then I realize that he called me "Mr. Dawson." My driver's license had my real name "Jason Powell" on it. He should not have known me by that name. My heart began to race as fear flooded my body. I had not been called by Warner's last name in nearly three years. I knew something was wrong and that I was in some serious trouble. He smiled at me and then asked:

"Do you remember me?"

"Yes sir, and I cannot thank you enough for only giving me a warning."

"No, not that. Do you remember me from before that?"

"No?"

"I was there the last time you saw your dad."

Suddenly I remembered him bursting through the front door of our house and arresting my dad. He was one of the officers that took Warner away after the Mobil Station arson.

Panic struck me as my past was suddenly sitting right in front of me, staring me in the face. I became terrified that he was going to judge me and treat me as though I was my dad, or even arrest me for a past crime. This math teacher/police officer, however, explained that he was proud of me for not becoming like my dad. He reassured me that I was a good person and not like Warner in any way. After Warner was taken away, this officer had begun secretly monitoring my behaviors at school.

He had taken it upon himself to watch out for me in case I needed any help adapting to my new life without a dad. Apparently, this man had been conversing with all of my teachers without my knowing, about my behaviors. He told me that he had witnessed my kindness, hard work, and passion for music. My growth in these areas were proof of my liberation and individuality apart from my dad. I never told the officer, but his words of approval meant the world to me.

While I was enjoying my new identity, I still had some heavy responsibilities. Due to my mom's size, she couldn't sleep in a regular bed. Rather, she slept on a single mattress placed on the floor. There was one day that she had rolled over a little and somehow became stuck between the mattress and the wall. The mattress compressed enough for her to get stuck so badly that I could not get her free. We eventually had to call 911 for help. A short while later, a firetruck arrived at our house to help. The firemen wedged a gurney between my mom and the wall and then attempted to roll her back onto the bed. As they pushed her with the gurney, the gurney suddenly cracked in half. Instantly, the firemen all burst into laughter. They couldn't believe that it had broken in half and openly laughed about it. They ran out to the truck to strap two more gurneys together so that they could try again. As they helped roll my mom over, I could see tears rolling down her cheeks. Her face was beet red from trying to hold in the tears. After they left, she broke into uncontrollable sobs.

"This was it. I'm done, I am now going to die," she said, looking at me helplessly.

"You're not going to die mom; you are just embarrassed. You will be ok."

"No, you are wrong. I'm done. There is nothing left for me in this world. I am now going to die. Please forgive me for your life. I'm sorry for all the things that happened to you."

Her stressful condition continued into the next morning. No matter what I said to reassure her that she was fine and that I forgave her, she would not listen. I had to leave for church, so I told her she would be fine and that I would be back in a couple of hours. After I left, she called a friend and asked her to help get her to the hospital. Because her friend worked at a storage place, she had access to a moving van she could use. She helped get my mom into the flat of a moving van and then took her to the hospital.

When they got to there, the nurses immediately admitted my mom into the hospital. Apparently one half of her heart had stopped working. Her lips were blue and she couldn't breathe—in short, *she really was dying*. Her friend drove back to tell me what was happening.

By the time I arrived, they had already sedated my mother. They allowed me to see her for a moment. She was laying down flat in a hospital bed with an air tube in her mouth. She lay there motionless with only the sound of the respirator and her heart monitor in the room. I tried telling the nurses that she could not breathe lying down and that they needed to sit her up. The weight of her body was too much on her lungs to breathe when she was lying down. They told me that it was ok because the machine was helping her. I tried to talk to her, but she didn't respond. It hurt my heart to see her like this and it felt weird and futile trying to talk to her when she was unconscious, and so, realizing I couldn't help her, I left.

I took care of my sisters all that week while we waited for my mom to get better. I didn't want my sisters to see their mom in the hospital bed, sedated and motionless. I didn't want to scare them or frighten them with such sights. I told them she would be better soon and home before Mother's Day.

After a week of waiting for some good news, the hospital called me and asked me to come meet with the doctor. I dropped my two older sisters off at school and left my youngest sister with a neighbor so that I could see what was wrong. When I got to the doctor's office, there was a priest waiting to talk with me. He was a tall thin black man with a bald head, dressed in a white dress shirt. He asked me to join him in a private room so that we could talk for a moment.

"Son, what do you believe happens to a person when they die?" he asked.

From what I had learned, I only had one answer, "They go to heaven or hell."

"Yes son, that is correct. You see, your mom is not going to get any better. She is going to die, but as long as we have her plugged into that machine, she is suffering. The machine is the only thing keeping her alive right now. You are the only person that can make this decision. But understand that every minute she is plugged into that machine, we are wasting tax dollars."

"So then, I need to unplug the machine?"

"You have to make the decision."

"Well, if she is going to die anyways, then we need to do it right?"

He motioned to the nurse with a nod of approval. The nurse pulled the tube out of my mom's mouth and then left the room. I sat there staring at my mom as she gasped for her final breaths for six minutes, twenty-two seconds. Then she took her last breath. My mom was barely thirty-six years old when she passed. It was a surreal feeling to think I wouldn't have her in my life anymore. But it didn't really affect me to watch her die. I never told anyone, but I had already been having dreams about her death for about two years.

After my dad was arrested, I started having nightmares once or twice a week where I would watch my mom gasp for air before dying. Sometimes she was being crushed under something or under water; while other times she would be choking or just simply couldn't breathe. By the time that it actually happened, I had already lived it countless times. I had already done all of my grieving years before; this was just the final step. I knew I had to close the curtain on the past.

Now What?

I went home that day and tried to explain to my sisters that their mom was not coming home. It was four days after Mother's Day, they missed her and wanted to see her. I did my best to explain death to her three little girls in a way that they would understand it. I was fortunate in the fact that my youth pastor was there to help me along every step of the way. He and his wife assisted me as I tried to explain to my sisters that they were never going to see their mom again.

"Girls, you know mom is with the doctors because she is really sick right?"

"Yes" they shook their heads.

I could tell at this moment that they knew something was wrong. Their eyes began to well up with tears as we each held a girl in our arms.

"Remember how mom used to cry a lot at night because her body hurt so badly? The doctors are not able to help fix her or stop the pain."

Their little chins began to quiver as they tried to stay strong.

"Mom asked Jesus if she could go to heaven early so that the pain would stop. She promised Jesus that she would help watch over us all to make sure we are safe."

My oldest sister tried her hardest to ask through her emotionally cracking voice.

"Mom is not coming home, is she?"

"No baby" I replied.

"Did she die?"

"Yes."

The girls had now begun crying, making it nearly impossible for me to stay strong for them. Despite the challenge, I kept my composure as I continued to try explaining to them.

"Mom loves you all very much, but she was hurting too much and wanted to help keep you guys safe. She said she could do that best for us from heaven. She wanted me to tell you that she would always be with you and that she would always be watching over you."

That night, after we all went to bed, I started to think over the events from that day. I started to believe that I had killed my own mother. After all, the priest at the hospital told me that I was the one who had to make the decision. I was the one who didn't believe her when she said she was going to die. *I made the choice.*

Although Warner was in prison, somehow, he had succeeded in killing my mother. He somehow succeeded in killing me as well in the process, as I would for sure be sent to prison now. He wasn't even in our lives anymore, yet somehow, I felt he still won. He managed to kill us all from behind bars.

The next morning, I went on auto pilot as I did what I always did. I still had to go to school, so I took my two older sisters to the local day care across from their elementary school. Unfortunately, my third sister, the baby, was only two years old. She was not old enough for the day care and so I took her to school with me.

My high school had a "locked out" policy where students were required to stand outside in the quad with a security officer if they missed the bell to class. Because I was late getting to school, my sister and I would have had to stand outside for this detention. I didn't want to stand in the sun with her, so I hid from security and walked around the buildings trying to hide in the shade. A security guard saw me and rode over on his bike.

"What are you doing?"

"I don't know."

"What are you doing, why are you out here with a baby?"

"I don't know, I Don't Know, I DON'T KNOW! It wasn't my fault! I didn't want her to die. I didn't want to kill her. He made me do it. It's not fair to blame me. I didn't want to kill her!"

In a state of panic, the security guard immediately called for back-up on his walkie-talkie. The police came to pick my sister and me up from the school. Being in a state of shock, I honestly don't remember a lot of what happened after this. I am not sure what happened to any of my sisters during this time. I do, however, remember sitting in a small room at the courthouse with groups of officer-like "official" men and women coming in and asking me a series of questions while videotaping me. As the questions proceeded, I began to feel more and more like a criminal being interrogated for his crimes. They asked me things about my dad, things about the people he hung out with. They asked about different crimes that they knew we were involved with but couldn't prove. At one point, they had my grandfather (the one who shot Warner) in the room listening. I don't know what they told him, what he heard, or what he knew; but I remember looking over and seeing him sobbing. I was terrified the whole time. They started asking me really odd questions that I didn't understand. They asked me several riddle-like questions about birds in a hand vs birds in a bush, amongst other tricky and thought-provoking questions. I don't know what the purpose of these questions was. In hindsight, I believe that they may have been gauging how I reacted to different scenarios, how I dealt with pressure, and if I could think logically. Basically, they were trying to see how traumatized I was.

The whole event was a whirlwind of confusion for me. All I know is that I made it abundantly clear that I wanted guardianship of my sisters. I grew up with Warner threatening me with horror stories about CPS, foster homes, group homes, and orphanages. I didn't want these things for my sisters. To protect them from these, I requested full guardianship of all three girls. Seeing as I had been raising them since birth already, it seemed it would be an easy task for me. After all, it was all any of us knew. I explained to the people interrogating me that I had been responsible for my sisters their whole lives. It hurt to say it out loud, but I actually felt that it would be easier now that my mom was dead, as it would just be the three girls and me.

The courts allowed me to continue taking care of my sisters until the day of the guardianship trial. During those following weeks, the people in my community all came to help us. They brought us food, helped with babysitting, helped us pay our bills, and encouraged us at every opportunity. My youngest sister would stay with a babysitter while my older sisters and I went to school. When I got home from school, I would pick up my youngest from the sitter and then we would go pick up the other two girls from their school. We appreciated the help, but I secretly felt ashamed that people felt they needed to come help us.

My sisters and I started to clean up the house. As much as it hurt to do so, we started removing all of my mom's stuff. I was hoping that if we erased her completely, then my sisters would no longer be reminded of their mother and the pain of losing her. Even still, they would often burst out crying without any warning as they thought about their mom. They missed her dearly. I did everything I could to comfort them, while trying to help them through their grief. I also missed her but had too much responsibility on my plate—mainly the welfare of my sisters—to dwell on thoughts of her.

Love & Verdicts?

For two long weeks we waited in anticipation for the court hearing to see what the future would hold. As intense as it was preparing for the guardianship trial, it was a much-needed closure to our few weeks of uncertainty. The two weeks leading up to the trial felt like an eternity of working aimlessly and imagining the best and worst outcome for us all, but not really knowing what would become of me or my sisters. Even more difficult was not knowing what to tell my sisters about what was going to happen. They always looked to me for answers, but at this moment I had none to give.

Finally, the day came where I stood in front of the judge. The fate of my sisters and I was in his hands. As the judge entered the courtroom, we all stood as instructed by the bailiff. Once we were all granted permission to sit, the judge stared motionless at me. His face was blank as a wall while the entire courtroom waited in silence, without moving a muscle for what felt like an eternity. I could feel the tension in the room as the judge sat—without emotion—staring into my soul. Suddenly the silence broke as the judge abruptly stood from his chair. Without hesitation, he started walking towards me from behind the bench. My heart raced, I could feel the sweat begin to gather on my back and I started to panic as the bailiff frantically reached for his firearm. The courtroom was cluttered with the sounds of the stenographer clicking away like crazy. Since I was not allowed to run, I didn't know what to do. As I sat there with my heart racing, I could sense something was very wrong as the entire courtroom filled with an odd sense of tension, anxiety, and excitement.

The judge walked over to where I was sitting and reached down as if he were picking me up like a child. Unsure of what was happening, I rose to my feet. He then wrapped his arms around me and held me for what felt like hours. I didn't understand what he was doing. Why was he hugging me, why did this stranger seem to care? Growing up as I did, I was not used to the care strangers might offer.

After his long embrace, he wiped tears from his eyes and then walked back to his chair. I looked around the room in confusion. There were so many people there that I recognized. My grandparents, my aunt and her family, my math teacher, random people from my community, people from church, and many more. These were the people whose care had helped me get to this point. As I glanced over the gathering in the room, I could see people drying their tears, wiping their noses, and smiling up at me with looks of approval. Almost too nervous to analyze what had just happened, I sat back in my chair in awe and wonderment.

I couldn't tell if the judge's hug meant that my sisters and I would stay together or if we were going to be separated into foster homes. I started to worry that perhaps I hadn't given the correct answers when they were interrogating me. Maybe my grades were not good enough, or worse, maybe they had reviewed my criminal record. Afterall, I was the child with a criminal record dating back to kindergarten. Did he know of the murders, the arsons, the unending thefts, and robberies? Why did the judge stare at me for so long before walking over to hug me?

Before my mind could race any further, the judge started reading testimonies from people who had stood up for me and my sisters. He read from a list of people who had all vouched in my stead that I not only could take care of my sisters but should be granted full guardianship. He said that the psychologists who were in the room asking me questions during my interrogation all supported that I was more than capable of continuing to raise my sisters. He said that the CPS (Child Protective Services) worker, who had checked up on us the week previous, had informed him that I was making great strides in cleaning and fixing the house and that I was showing the full potential to become a good caretaker for my sisters.

In short, the judge granted me full guardianship of my three half-sisters. He warned me that what I was requesting would be one of the hardest things I would ever do and that I would be giving up all opportunities to live a normal life by taking on this responsibility. I had insisted that it would be unfair to my sisters to be sent to foster homes or orphanages after the death of their mother and incarceration of their father.

Ultimately, the judge said that I was an inspiration and that he wished me the best of luck. He encouraged me to surround myself with lots of people who could help me whenever I had questions or needed to reach out for assistance or advice. I had not yet even graduated high school, but on that day, in that courtroom, I became the legal guardian of three little girls. I was now responsible for a nine-year-old, an eight-year-old, and two-year-old.

For the first time in my life, I had real hope. As much as I loved my mom, this was the day that I was finally granted *real freedom* from my past. With Warner still in prison and my mom now dead, I had the chance with my sisters to start my life all over. I had a chance to provide them with the life that I never had, a life better than their mother could have ever offered.

After granting me custody of my sisters, the judge wanted to help us as much as he could. He wrote up and served a restraining order against Warner. Upon his future release from prison, this restraining order would prohibit Warner from ever entering the county we lived in. The judge also set me up with a specialized case worker who would help me with everything I needed before leaving the courts that day.

This case worker helped me to enroll into government assistance programs so that we would start receiving monthly aid from Welfare, WIC, and Supplemental Security Income (SSI). They also helped me sign up for Medi-Cal, college financial aid, and a program that paid for any childcare I needed so that I could go to school and get a job. We didn't receive a lot of money every month, but it was enough for a family of kids who had never really had any money, to start working towards success.

A Brother's Love & Protection

Over the years, my parents had never paid the property taxes on the mobile home that we lived in. We had started receiving letters from the county notifying us that we were in danger of losing the house. With the help of my grandparents, I was able to pay the back taxes ensuring that I could continue to live there with the girls. However, the house still remained an absolute mess.

My youngest sister had now been diagnosed with lead poisoning. Because Warner used to boil the lead from car batteries over the stove in the kitchen, we all had been in danger of lead poisoning. Someone told me that a good thorough cleaning of the house would help get rid of the lead poisoning. With the help of my friends and neighbors, we immediately began the ultimate clean up. We spent weeks of our summer break scraping the paint off all the windows, scrubbing the walls, ripping out the carpets, and basically re-building the house from the ground up.

I rented a dumpster to throw away everything that was unsafe or reminded me of Warner. As we removed items from the house and threw them into the dumpster, we would throw the things into it as hard as we could, trying to break them. This was one of the most therapeutic events a victim turned survivor like me could ask for. With every change I made and every piece I tore out, I could feel myself erasing even more of Warner from our lives. It was a long and hard process, but I enjoyed every moment.

My mom died two weeks before my high school graduation. By the time I officially graduated, I was already named the official guardian of my three little sisters. I had no idea what I was going to do, but I knew I was going to have to make some decisions. Because the courts signed me up for programs that paid for childcare and college, I figured I should at least try attending college.

Luckily for me, my youth pastor's mother-in-law worked at the local community junior college. She helped me enroll at the College of the Desert. When I met with her, I didn't know what I wanted to major in. She encouraged me to try culinary arts since that was one of the only classes I liked in high school. Truth be told, I only liked the culinary class in high school because I had a crush on a girl in that class. All the same, not being sure of what lay ahead for a career, culinary classes sounded great to me.

The college aide who was helping me enroll asked me what classes I wanted to take. I had no idea, so I signed up for twenty-four units' worth of classes. She laughed and told me it was too much, but that I could try each class out to see what I liked. Because twelve units was considered a full load of classes, she said we would drop the classes I didn't like after the first week. She also helped sign me up for more financial aid programs like EOPS and Work Study.

Going to college was the first time in my life that no one knew who I was. No one was able to judge me for my past because no one knew me. I was so excited to be there, to prove myself, to become something more. And I thrived in every class I took. I ended up keeping all twenty-four units while maintaining straight A's! The college allowed me to keep taking as many units as I wanted as long as I could keep good grades, which I did. They allowed me to continue taking twenty-four units, every semester, for all four years that I was there.

There was a work study program at the college that got me a job in a local bakery where I worked for nine years in total. My boss, "Chef" became like a big sister to me. She encouraged and helped me with anything and everything I could have ever asked. She not only taught me to bake, but also good work ethic. In addition, she was there to help me if I needed a loan, advise, or just simple encouragement as I continued to work, go to school, and raise a family.

It was during this time that I married my first wife. Although we were young, we found a way to raise my sisters. On the weekdays, we would drop the girls off at school before going to school and then work. After school, the girls would go to day care until one of us got home to pick them up. On the weekends, I would work on Saturday, then we would spend time together as a family. On Sundays, we would all go to church together.

Towards the end of my second year of college, a friend invited me to see the college's percussion ensemble classes' final concert. The experience of seeing this concert was an absolute life-changing, transformational, and monumental moment for me! I watched the percussionists as they skillfully read the music on the page and played a variety of different percussion instruments. I didn't want to miss a second of what I was seeing and so my heart raced as I fought away the need to blink my eyes. In that moment, I felt as though my entire life had come to a screeching halt of realization. This was my calling; this was my future. I asked one of the students after the concert how they did all of that.

"It's easy, just take the class. We meet on Thursday nights. You should join us. You will love it."

I spent the rest of that semester and my winter break thinking about nothing else. As soon as course selections became available for the next semester, I signed up for the class and LOVED IT! After taking the percussion class, I continued my music studies by taking every music class the college had to offer. I completed my culinary arts associate degree, then spent two additional years as a music major in the community college before being accepted to the University of Redlands for Music Education.

Luckily, this university had a program that allowed me to live at home and commute in for my classes. I was able to continue working and raising my girls just as I had done while attending my junior college. Because I was a transfer student with an associate degree, I only had to attend the university for three years in total.

The Real Beginning

There is a lot that happened in the following years. I made many mistakes as I fought my way through learning to be an adult. I married my first wife a few months after getting guardianship of my sisters. We raised all three girls the best we could; and had two children of our own during that time. Our marriage did not last, but we get along well enough to co-parent our two children.

I was able to provide my sisters with a stable home environment. They each were able to become good citizens and successful adults in their own life choices. All three girls not only graduated high school but also went on to college. I don't know how much they remember of their mom or dad. I know they have a few bad memories of some of the painful events, but I'd like to believe that they don't remember much of those awful times. Luckily, I think they were young enough for most of those memories to fade away with time.

Warner was released from prison several years after my mom's death. With exception of two times, we have done a good job of avoiding Warner at all costs. The girls have no interest in ever getting together to meet him. They said that their lives were better without him, so why give him the chance to ruin their lives now? They have all grown into successful women with families of their own.

Throughout those nine years I kept working at the bakery, and made enough money to support my family while I continued my educational goals as a music major. I also gave private music lessons and led worship in a local church during that time to help supplement the cost of raising three little girls, supporting my wife, and raising our own two children.

I spent four years in total at my first community college. During which, I accomplished three culinary certificates, my AA in Culinary Management, and all my required transfer units for a music major in the university. I held the honor of "Dean's List" the entire time I was there, received many scholarships, and was awarded the Rotary-Alumni award for Instrumental Excellence.

After exhausting every music course available, I had to move on to the next level of my education. I felt that I was still a baby musician and feared I was not good enough for university level music. Because of this concern, I continued my education at a different community college (Riverside Community College) for one more additional year. After this additional year, one of my teachers encouraged me to— at least—audition for my first-choice university for the experience. To my surprise, I was not only accepted as a transfer student, but I also received many scholarships.

I spent three years in total, student teaching included, at the University of Redlands earning my bachelor's degree in music education with a California teaching credential. I was extremely lucky in the fact that I was hired by my first student teaching placement, so I had a job already lined up after graduation to teach symphonic orchestra, classical guitar, and choir at a high school.

Since I didn't want to stop learning, I continued at the university to earn a master's degree in guitar performance. After one year of trying to balance a career, a family, and a performance degree; I had to switch to a different major. I decided to switch universities altogether to earn my master's in music education. I completed my master's degree and figured I might as well continue on to earn a doctorate degree. I continued teaching full time while attending the universities for all three degrees. It was a lot of hard work, but I successfully completed three certificates, two associates, a bachelor's, master's, and doctorate by the fifteenth year after graduating high school.

I also successfully raised all three girls, bought a home, established my career, and raised my own two children. During this time, I traveled all over the world, visited over 30 different countries, received two "Teacher of the Month" recognitions, and was nominated for many awards, including making it into the quarterfinals of the "Grammy School's Music Educator Award." I was also inducted into the "Alumni of the Year" Hall of Fame at my first community college. After growing up in a world where I was the unwanted burden, a red-headed stepchild, I sought and succeeded in making something more of myself and my life.

*

I've seen Warner two times since the day he was arrested. The first time was a few years after graduating high school when he was released from prison. He reached out to me to get a ride from the bus station to a halfway home. I gave him the ride but was pretty quiet the whole time. I didn't want him to know anything about his daughters or myself. I was afraid that he would try to sneak his way back into our lives to destroy us again.

The second time I saw him was after he somehow learned that I was granted full guardianship of his daughters. He asked if he could meet them and maybe give them a good impression/memory of who their dad was. At first, I was resistant, but then he explained that he had developed throat cancer and was given only a few months to live.

I drove my sisters out to meet their dad, just in case he was telling the truth and really was dying. Still, I suspected that he was lying and only wanted to guilt trip us into allowing him to enter our lives. Having seen him perform this trick many times before, I had a feeling that this was his way of trying to eventually regain his control over us. All the same, we spent one afternoon with him. It was a long and uncomfortable afternoon for us, but we made it through. At the end of our visit, he hugged us all and told us he loved us and hoped we could stay in touch. We did not!

It was not until days after I defended my doctoral dissertation, fifteen years later that I heard from him one last time. I answered a random call one night:

"Hi Jake."

My heart sank when I heard his voice. I had not been "Jake" in over fifteen years. I could feel my legs begin to shake as my heart pounded. My eyes welled up with tears as my chin quivered with fear. I don't know how he got my number, but here he was calling me. We only talked for about a minute in total. During that minute, he told me thirty minutes worth of information. It sounded like he was back on speed again as his words raced through the phone. The whole time he sped through the lifetime of words, he kept mentioning his four years in the Chino prison for child molestation.

When the phone call ended, I told my new wife that it felt as though he was trying to ask for forgiveness for only that one event. I was so insulted that he didn't care about anything else he had done. Through all the years of horrible abuses he imposed on my mom and me, his only concern was the child molestation account with the young girl that had got him convicted. I told my wife that it felt as though (in his head) this one event was the peak of his crimes. If he could achieve forgiveness for this one thing, all other things would be erased because this was the worst of them. It was not the worst of them, but it was the one thing that impacted *his life* the most. It felt as though he disregarded all the other egregious abuses he imposed on my mother and me because he never served time in prison for them. The only crime he needed forgiveness for was the one that he served real time for.

I have not seen or heard from him since that call. I "Google" him once in a while to see if there is anything new. From what I have seen, he is still alive and living in a town not far from me. This does make me a little nervous, but I am not too worried. The judge who gave me guardianship of my sisters also put a restraining order against him which extends throughout the entire county. He could break the restraining order by entering our county, but I don't think he has any desire to find me now. His daughters are all grown, and we have all moved on. I think he knows we want nothing to do with him, giving him no reason to even try reaching out to us again. I did change his name in this book as a means of protection for my sisters and me.

DNA & Facebook

After learning that Warner was not my actual father and that I was an actual red headed stepchild, I started asking my mom who my real father was. She would never tell me anything about him. I believe that she was fearful for everyone involved. If his identity got out, who knows what Warner might do. It wasn't until the last few months of her life that she told me my biological father's name. She didn't know anything that would help me find him, but she did give me a name. I wanted to reach out and try to find this person, but I feared I would come off as "needing" or "wanting" if I found him right after my mom's death. Because of this, I waited until after I completed my bachelor's degree and had a steady career before I tried to find him.

My mother had only told me his name, with no location, age, description, or an accurate spelling of his last name. I figured since I was born in San Diego, he must have been from that area. I tried reaching out to every man with the name she gave me, or a name even relatively close to that, in the San Diego area. After a few months with no results, I gave up.

I tried again a few years later after completing my master's degree. And once again, I was unsuccessful. It wasn't until years later, after completing my doctorate that I tried one last time. This time I got smart and sent a message out as follows:

To whom it may concern, my name is Dr. Jason Powell, and I am in search of a man by your name in regard to the late Jenny Anne. Upon her death bed, she asked me to locate a gentleman with your name from the San Diego Area. This person would have known her around 1980. If you are this person, please reach out to me.

To my surprise, a man did reach out to me on Facebook Messenger. "I remember Jenny. She had a beautiful smile," he wrote.

With so many scams that happen on social media, I had to ask further. "Can you tell me anything else about her?"

"You mean, can I prove that I actually knew her?"

"Yes," I responded.

He immediately sent me a picture of my mom. It was a picture of her with her foster sister and best friend. I was shocked that I may have actually found my biological father. I quickly looked him up on Facebook to see a picture of him. It was somewhat startling to see the similarities between the two of us, as we look nearly identical. I could see right away that we had the same forehead, eyes, and cheeks. I sent a reply:

"If I am not mistaken, you two may have dated for a while?"

"LOL, I guess you could say that!"

"Well, "LOL," I am the result of your "dating." I am your son. Don't worry, I don't want anything from you, I only want to know about your health. Is there anything in your family that I should be aware of?"

"Wait, what? You are my son? I want to meet you."

*

We did meet and did get a genetic/DNA test done. There was a 100% match. As it turns out, I have an entire family on his side. I now have two half-brothers, grandparents, aunts, uncles, cousins, and much more. After years of being isolated and imprisoned under Warner's roof, I now had more family than I know what to do with. As of now, we have all had a wonderful five-year long relationship and look forward to many more. My Bio-dad and I have more things in common than I could ever list. We talk on the phone every week and visit each other at least once every other month.

I understand why my mom never told me about my dad. I think she knew that if Warner ever found out who he was, he would have probably tried to kill him. Warner is a scary guy with no moral code. If he decided to find this guy, he most likely would have done something bad. I think my mom kept the identity of my father a secret to keep him safe. After all, Warner is the man who did a drive-by shooting in an attempt of killing his own family.

Closure

So why have I shared my life story? Why do I make myself vulnerable to the world by sharing some of the horrible things Warner did to me? I am not proud of those crimes I participated in with Warner during my youth. I am not proud of the horrifying things he did and/or made me do. I have only shared small portions of what he actually did to us, but even these little bits are embarrassing and hard to share. The stories in this book, although horrifying, sadly are not the worst parts of the horrors I have locked away in my head. There are parts of my past I will never share with anyone. I am beyond embarrassed of the filth that I keep locked away. Yet here I am sharing vast chunks anyways . . . and you may be wondering why.

I realized early in my teaching career that many of my students are going through horrible situations at home that they are terrified and too embarrassed or scared to share. These students could possibly be fighting through many of the same abuses I lived through. These unfortunate kids have no one to look to for help and so I started sharing my "story" on the last day of high school for the seniors. I call it my "Powell Pep Talk."

I explain to the students that no matter how bad life may seem, there is a future waiting for them, and that life can get better. I share some of my stories and then share the key lessons that I have learned through my life so far. I have become somewhat of an "inspirational motivator" for my students. My wife points out to me often that I am an inspirational motivator to many more people than just my students. She continues to tell me that there are many people out there who could benefit from my learned experiences. I share this with you all because if relating my horrible past can yield a positive outcome for anyone who hears it, even if it's just one person, then it makes the whole experience of reviewing the past a little more worthwhile. I share this in hopes that you, the reader, can be motivated and encouraged to do amazing things with your own lives, despite the hardships some of you may have to face.

I could easily argue that my life was worse than what most people live through. I could blame my parents for what I lived through. I could have given up on life and played the "victim card," but the truth is that it would only hurt me and my loved ones. If I can pull myself together after having been thrown into a Safeway dumpster—beaten, broken, worthless and unwanted— into the person I am today, then we all have no right to be anything less than absolutely amazing!

If you look at a person for what they are,

that's what they'll remain.

But if you look at a person for what they could be,

that's what they'll become.

-Dr. Jason Powell

Discussion Questions for The Author

- **Are these stories all really true?** Yes, every story I have shared is in its absolute truest form. Before publishing this book, I had many people from my past read through it to ensure my memories have not drifted in any way. Every person who was present for any of my stories has confirmed with me that I am sharing nothing but the absolute truth.

- **How did you make it through all of this?** Honestly, I survived because I had to. I had to be strong for my sisters. I was so focused on protecting them that I never had time to dwell on my own misfortunes. When you combine this with the fact that I truly hate everything that Warner was, I have no choice but to survive. I live my life now trying to prove to everyone that I am not Warner, and that I am a worthy individual.

- **Are you and your sisters really OK now?** Yes. As hard as it is to believe, we are all truly grateful for the horrid past we share. It is not a traditional model of a healthy childhood, but it drove each of us to become more than what we were. We all share the same driving passion never to be anything like Warner. Because of this, we all work hard to be positive, uplifting, hard-working, devoted members of society.

- **Did the judge actually tell your grandpa to go practice shooting more?** Yes, this actually happened. The entire courtroom snickered when he said this to my grandfather. It's hard to understand, but the entire county we lived in hated Warner. Everyone knew who he was, and everyone hated him. The judge was being straight forward and honest when he told him that. There were so many times the police had to come arrest Warner, only to have him out walking the streets again a day later. The man was an unstoppable force.

- **Why didn't you just run away?** I would never have been able to run away leaving my sisters behind with Warner. I would have had to take them with me. I truly believe that if he had ever caught me trying to sneak his daughters away from him, he would have beat me death. In my head, running away was never a possibility for us.

- **Do you want to confront Warner?** No. I have absolutely no desire to ever see or hear from him again. I am still to this day absolutely terrified of Warner. Even as a grown man, I don't know that I have the courage to ever confront him.

- **How did CPS not take you kids away?** It is extremely rare that CPS is able to take a child from their mother. Because my mom was there and I would lie about my home conditions, they never had the opportunity to remove us.

- **Where was your family after your mom died?** I was so afraid of my sisters being split apart and sent to foster homes that I basically blocked anyone from coming too close to us. I never allowed anyone from my family to step in and take the girls from me. My mother told me once that she wanted us to stay together after she died. I fought to make her wish come true by only allowing people to come in and help, not take over. My grandparents and aunt all respected our wishes. They were only a phone call away if we needed them, otherwise, they let me raise my girls without conflict.

- **How did your mom and sisters live through pregnancies with Warner around?** Whenever my mom was pregnant, Warner would direct all of his anger towards me. He would treat her significantly better during her pregnancies to assure his children were protected. The irony was that he would still drink, smoke, and do drugs with my mom when she was pregnant.

- **How was your mom obese if you never had food in the house?** When I was young, my mother snuck out to the car one night. My dad followed her out and found her eating a box of Cracker jacks. He beat her within an inch of her life. She told me later that he had been starving her for several months because he wanted a "skinny wife." She struggled with weight her whole life, but his controlling demeaner forced her to sneak foods behind his back. Unfortunately, these foods were always horribly unhealthy. Many people don't understand that healthy foods cost significantly more than "junk food." For example, a bottle of water at a convenience store can cost up to $4.00, where as a 32oz Slurpee can cost as little as $0.79.

- **What did your parents do all day?** When they were high, my dad would take things apart in his garage while my mom did the same in her bedroom. Or they would simply leave for a few days. When they were "coming down" from their high, they would sleep for days at a time. They never really accomplished or did anything significant. There were a lot of days wasted waiting for opportunities to steal, hurt, and get more drugs.

- **Didn't your teachers ever notice and report any markings on you?** There were many times that my teachers would call CPS on my dad. Unfortunately, CPS has a really hard time taking children away from their mothers. Because my mother was there with us, there really was not a whole lot that CPS could do to help. After CPS would leave, Warner would beat us without remorse. My teachers all learned pretty quickly that reporting us only hurt us more.

- **Did you go through years of therapy?** I have never been to therapy for any of my past. I have been very fortunate to be surrounded by loving and caring people who have always been there to help motivate and lift me up. Because like-minded people tend to group together, I have been surrounded by positive and hard-working people. Also, I keep myself too busy to have time to dwell on the past.

- **Have you ever tried to find the people who helped you so that you could tell them you made it through?** I have tried reaching out too many of the "key people" from my life to thank them. My youth pastor and I are still very close and so he knows my story and how much I appreciate him. I am still in contact with my old neighbor who helped call 911 when my grandfather shot Warner. She knows my story and my appreciation for her. Unfortunately, most of the others have either passed away or I simply cannot locate them. I cannot locate the judge who gave me guardianship. The officer/math teacher passed away towards the end of Covid. The guidance counselor at the community college passed away several years back. My grandfather, aunt, and her husband all passed away many years ago as well. But all of them showed up in divine timing when I needed them, and I am eternally grateful.

- **Have you shared your past with your children?** My babies are my life and so I have kept my past somewhat of a secret from them. I wanted them to have the best childhood possible, so I kept as much darkness out of their sight as I could. Once in high school, I feel they are old enough to maturely process the things they hear. My son was a freshman last year and so he got to hear my "Powell Pep Talk" story at the end of the year. He is aware of many of the horrors I have overcome, and the triumphs that followed. My daughter is a freshman this year and so she will be hearing my story for the first time at the end of the year.

It Takes A Village

I would like to acknowledge the people who helped save my life and that of my three sisters

To my youth pastor: Thank you for never giving up on me. You are by far the closest thing I had to a dad in my childhood. You were the one who believed in me and my future. You were always there to encourage and support me. You are honestly, one of the biggest reasons I am who I am today and was able to break free from my past.

To my best friend: Thank you for always being there with me. I don't know that I ever shared a whole lot of what was happening at home. But for the little bit I did share, you were always there to help me press through. You were my only true friend. No matter how many miles, no matter how many years go by, I'll always be willing to mail you a curly fry from Jack in the Box.

To my second mom (My best friend's mother): Thank you for letting me and my sisters escape to your house so often, and for putting up with your son and me whenever we were behaving like typically dumb teenage boys. I know we were a pain in the butt sometimes. Also, thank you for always being a good friend to my mom. You truly meant a lot to her as she didn't really have many friends.

To my chef at the bakery: Thank you for being more than a boss. You helped me learn how to be an adult while always encouraging me to strive for more. Your flexibility on my hours made it possible to raise my sisters and still go to school while working. You literally made my life possible.

To my dissertation committee: Thank you both for helping me through my dissertation. It's because of your help and support that I was able to complete an autoethnography. If not for my dissertation, I would not be sitting here writing this.

To my neighbor in 6th grade: Thank you for always being there ready to help. No matter what the abuses were in my house, you were always there, willing, and ready to help us escape. The countless times you stood up for us, helped us get to abuse shelters, and supported us, will never be forgotten. Your love and compassion were a huge part of our survival.

To my grandparents: Thank you for everything you were able to help with. No matter how messed up life was for us, you were always the safety net that we could run to. You helped me in more ways than I could express.

To my other best friend and editor: Thank you for your endless friendship and support. It means more than you know to have a guy friend I can be dumb with, as well as one who could help with all the edits needed in my early drafts.

To my ex-wife: I know I didn't really mention you in this book. I promise this was out of respect for you and your life. Please know that I appreciate everything you did in helping me to raise the girls. We were both far too young to take on such a challenge, but we did it anyways.

To my sisters: I don't know that I would have stayed alive if not for you three. I had no intention of letting Warner continue to hurt me, so I probably would have ended my own life. Once you were born and I started living as your "protector," I began working my way towards freedom. I am so proud of you three and cannot thank you enough for making it through with me.

To my children: Thank you both. You are all of my hopes and dreams combined. I could not be any prouder of anyone ever.

To my wife: Thank you for your endless love and support. You make me a better person. You push me to new levels and never allow me to be anything less than the best I can be.

Made in United States
Troutdale, OR
11/02/2023

14243374R00146